THE CASE FOR

Fr
CHARLES DOMINIC FFRENCH
(1775-1851)

*For Father Jackman,
Here is a book about a
Dominican to a Dominican.
With warm wishes
Donna Morell
Lary Desmond.*

THE CASE FOR

Fr
CHARLES DOMINIC FFRENCH
(1775-1851)

Lawrence A. Desmond
and
Donna M. Norell

Laverdure & Associates
Historians & Publishers

2004

© Lawrence A. Desmond and Donna M. Norell 2004

All rights reserved

No part of this publication may be reproduced, stored in a retrieval system, or transmitted in any form or by any means, electronic, mechanical, photocopying, recording, or otherwise, without prior permission of the copyright owners.

Library and Archives Canada Cataloguing in Publication

Desmond, Lawrence A.
The case for Fr Charles Dominic Ffrench (1775-1851) / Lawrence A. Desmond and Donna M. Norell

Includes bibliographical references and index.
ISBN 0-9688813-6-X

1. Ffrench, Charles Dominic, 1775-1851. 2. Dominicans–Biography. 3. Catholic Church–New Brunswick–Clergy–Biography. 4. Catholic Church–Maine–Clergy–Biography. 5. Clergy–New Brunswick–Biography. 6. Clergy–Maine–Biography. I. Norell, Donna M., 1932- II. Title.

BX4705.F44D48 2004　　　　　　　　　　　　282'.092
C2004-905680-8

For further copies or information on this or other fine publications about the religious history of Canada, please contact:

> Laverdure & Associates
> Historians & Publishers
> 194 Second Avenue North
> Yorkton, Saskatchewan
> S3N 1G7 Canada
>
> drpaul@sasktel.net
> tel. & fax 1-306-783-1832

This book has been published with the financial assistance of the Diocese of Saint John, of St. Thomas University through the auspices of its Pope John XXIII Chair of Studies in Catholic Theology, and of an anonymous clerical benefactor.

Printed and bound in Canada

This book is dedicated to the memory of
Vincent Joseph Jensen S.J.
(1916-1988)

CONTENTS

Abbreviations 9
Acknowledgements 11
Introduction 13
Chapter 1. Ffrench's Early Years:
  Ireland and Portugal (1775-1812) 23
Chapter 2. A Small Taste of Success: Quebec and New
  Brunswick (1812-1816) 33
Chapter 3. Trials and Setbacks:
  New Brunswick (1816-1818) 55
Chapter 4. Troubles with Trusteeism:
  New York (1818-1820) 65
Chapter 5. *Roma locuta est, causa finita est:*
  New York (1820-1822) 79
Chapter 6. Discoveries and Disappointments:
  New Brunswick (1822-1826) 93
Chapter 7. Final Projects: New England, Rome,
  New Brunswick (1826-1851) 115
Chapter 8. The Role of Nationalism in the Case
  Against Fr Ffrench 129
Chapter 9. Fr Ffrench's Case and the Passage
  of Time 151

Appendix A. "A Short Memoir, with some Documents in Vindication of the Charges made by Malicious Persons Against the Character of the Rev. Charles Ffrench, addressed to the Roman Catholics of British America, and of the United States." Saint John, 5 Aug. 1822 161

Appendix B. "The Conversion of Charles Ffrench to the Catholic Church." Rome, 26 April 1840 175

Appendix C. Petition of Charles Dominic Ffrench to His Holiness Pope Gregory XVI. 28 July 1840 ... 188

Appendix D. "Details sur la Province de la Nouvelle Brunswick par Fr. Charles Dominique Ffrench ordre des Précheurs." [1840] 189

Bibliography 193

Index of Persons and Rural Localities 203

ABBREVIATIONS

VA		Vatican Archives
	ANL	Archivo Nunzatura Lisbona
APF		Archivio della Sacra Congregazione 'de Propaganda Fide'
	LDNA	Scritture Riferite nei Congressi S.C. America Settentrionale, Canada, Nuova Bretagna, Labrador, Terra Nuova [on cover of each volume: Letters and Documents Concerning North America], copies held in St. Paul's College Library at the University of Manitoba, uncatalogued
	SOCG	Scritture Originali Riferite nelle Congregazioni Generali
	SOCG-SP	Scritture Originali Riferite nelle Congregazioni Generali [on cover of each volume: Sacr. Cong. de Prop. Fide], copies held in St. Paul's College Library at the University of Manitoba, uncatalogued
	Acta	Acta
	L e D	Lettere e Decreti
AAB		Archives of the Archdiocese of Boston

AABalt	Archives of the Archdiocese of Baltimore
AAD	Archives of the Archdiocese of Dublin
AAQ	Archives de l'Archevêché de Québec
RL	Registre des lettres
NB	Nouveau-Brunswick
NE	Nouvelle-Ecosse
EU	Etats-Unis
IPE	Île-du-Prince-Edouard
TN	Terre-Neuve
ADC	Archives of the Diocese of Charlottetown
ADSJ	Archives of the Diocese of Saint John
TA	Archives of the Irish Dominican Province, Tallaght, Co. Dublin

References given in the footnotes are those under which the documents were obtained or consulted.

ACKNOWLEDGEMENTS

This study could not have been brought to fruition without the participation of many persons. The authors wish especially to express their gratitude to the many archivists, librarians and friends who have lent a helping hand along the way. Particular thanks go to Hugh Fenning O.P., Dr Angelo Gualtieri, Fr Bernard M. Broderick, Fr Theodore Reznowski, Professor Cristina Povoledo, the late C.P. Forster O.P., and the late Leonard E. Boyle O.P., for their valuable advice and assistance with textual matters; to Fr Alex Baran for his past diligence in obtaining a large collection of Propaganda Fide documents for St. Paul's College; to Dr Richard Lebrun for his advice and encouragement; to Mrs Elizabeth Cann and the late Mrs Jane Lodge Smith for their navigational help in the New Brunswick Museum Archives; and above all to the staff of St. Paul's College Library at the University of Manitoba–Ms Georgina Lewis, Mr Bill Wsiaki, Ms Barb Unger, the late Ms Rosemary Dwyer, and the late Harold Drake S.J.–for their never-failing courtesy, patience and willing efforts on our behalf.

Finally, we should like to express our profound gratitude to St. Thomas University, under the auspices of its Pope John XXIII Chair of Studies in Catholic Theology, to an anonymous clerical benefactor, and to the Diocese of Saint John for their generous financial support of this project.

St. Paul's College
University of Manitoba
Winnipeg

View of the Miramichi, c. 1760, by Paul Sandby after Hervey Smyth, retouched by Peter Paul Benazech. Courtesy New Brunswick Museum, Saint John, N.B. (W1097).

INTRODUCTION

In the spring of 1817, the Irish Dominican, Fr Charles Dominic Ffrench, was lingering in Saint John, New Brunswick, convalescing and awaiting more propitious travelling conditions before setting out for New York, where, he hoped, the milder climate would restore his fragile health. He had already received his exeat, as well as cordial wishes for his future well-being, from Bishop Joseph-Octave Plessis of the Diocese of Quebec, under whom he had laboured as missionary for some four years. While he was thus waiting, his colleague, Fr Joseph Morisset[1] of Bartibog, wrote to Bishop Plessis informing him of a rumour that Fr Ffrench had been accused of fathering a child in the Miramichi area.

Fr Morisset had not waited to inquire into the rumour. He had written to the bishop within twenty-four hours of hearing the gossip. Nor did Bishop Plessis investigate the matter, either then or later. Instead, he wrote to Ffrench, revoking all but his most basic powers throughout the diocese, and giving no word of explanation. Bowing submissively to Plessis' verdict, the bewildered Ffrench, who as yet knew nothing about the accusation, naturally sought to know the reason. Yet the bishop refused to give any and, indeed, quickly ceased communicating directly with Ffrench altogether.

Once in New York, Fr Ffrench became involved in the struggle with trusteeism, taking the side of Bishop John Connolly against the trustees. By doing so, he acquired some

---

[1] Some documents and critical articles spell the name "Morissette," but we have adopted the spelling used in Fr Morisset's own signature, which is quite clear in his letters to Archbishop Plessis.

powerful enemies, who sought vigorously to discredit him. The rumour from Canada was invoked, and embroidered upon. In addition, other grave accusations, all false, were made against him. Because of these, however, Fr Ffrench was placed in the impossible situation of proving that the accusations, which had developed from incidents occurring or statements made in Ireland, Portugal and Canada, were untrue. In 1820, Rome stepped into the quarrel between the bishop and the trustees, in an effort to restore peace to the New York diocese. Although documents show that Rome by no means believed that Ffrench was guilty of the charges against him, or that he had played a negative part in the battle for power in New York, Propaganda decreed that, for the sake of peace, both he and his principal clerical opponent, Fr Pierre Malou, should leave the diocese. Fr Malou refused and was suspended, then expelled from his Order, and later reinstated. Fr Ffrench took advantage of the situation to travel to New Brunswick in an effort to clear his name, arriving there in 1822.

And clear it he did, or should have, so far as any reasonable reviewer of all the evidence is concerned. Petitions, testaments of good character, revocations by rumour mongers: Ffrench and his supporters sent a whole battery of documents to Plessis, now raised to the rank of archbishop. Plessis did not even deign to reply. His correspondence shows that he even referred to Ffrench as the cause of all the troubles in New York, despite the fact that the struggle with trusteeism had been in full swing long before Ffrench's arrival there.

Discouraged, Ffrench returned to the United States in 1826, where he took service under Bishop Benedict Fenwick of Boston. He remained in New England until his death in 1851, breaking his missionary service there for a year or so towards 1839-1840, in order to travel to Ireland, Rome and Saint John. During his many years in the United States, his work drew praise from superiors and parishioners alike. Upon his death, eulogies stressed charity and forgiveness as being his chief virtues.[2]

But in Canada especially, the damage was already done. Fr Ffrench's reputation as an immoral and troublesome priest remained largely unchallenged among historians for over one hundred and fifty years. Even in recent decades, he has usually been labelled negatively, both insofar as his personal life is concerned as well as with respect to the role he played in New York church politics. This is, of course, partly because documentary evidence was for many years difficult to obtain, either for conviction or for acquittal of the charges against him. And, in Canada, the categorical rejection of him by a prelate so esteemed as Archbishop Plessis, whose refusal to hear Ffrench's case was re-affirmed by Archbishop Bernard Claude Panet on the grounds that it had already been judged by his predecessor, was sufficient in the eyes of most, to ensure that Fr Charles Dominic Ffrench be adjudged as morally beyond the pale.

The authors of this book are convinced, however, that Fr Ffrench's negative reputation is for the most part undeserved. The present study therefore undertakes, first, to make a thorough presentation of Fr Ffrench's experiences in Canada and in New York—something that has never before been done—including a summary of the events in Ireland and Portugal that engendered some of the accusations against him; secondly, to assess the arguments for and against his innocence of the various charges; thirdly, to indicate why all the factual evidence was not taken into account during his lifetime, including the role that nationalism may have played in pertinent events in both Canada and the United States; fourthly, to trace briefly the principal channels of historical criticism whereby Fr Ffrench's reputation has been perpetuated; and, finally, to re-affirm the conclusions to which the evidence presented has led us.

---

[2] *Boston Pilot*, March 1851, "The Late C.D. Ffrench"; AAB Memoranda, 7 Jan. 1851.

16 *The Case for Fr Charles Dominic Ffrench (1775-1851)*

Aims and Purposes

The most striking discovery made during our research into the Fr Ffrench case has been, of course, that of the depth and ramifications of the injustice perpetrated. Not only was Fr Ffrench's reputation unjustly tarnished, the tarnish acquired additional layers of obfuscation as the years passed. His story constitutes a good case study of how, in the early nineteenth century in Canada, a Roman Catholic missionary could be falsely accused and the injustice not only be allowed to stand but be encouraged to flourish. Though Fr Ffrench was never a high-profile member of the hierarchy, in the interests of historical truth such a situation should not be allowed to continue indefinitely. It is important that the wrongs of the past be redressed, the truth be published, and history be corrected.

We should like to point out that this book is not written in an effort to whitewash or make a hero out of a nonentity. Nor is it about a rebel priest. It is a book that highlights tensions and problems within the Canadian Church during a certain period in the past, tensions of which Fr Ffrench's case is a prime illustration. It is also a book about Canadian justice, in particular ecclesiastical justice, and about a wrong that should have been righted long ago. Nor can such justice be fully achieved by presenting the case in summary fashion in a couple of articles without adequate context. It requires thorough and intensive treatment presented in a cohesive manner, and with all supporting documents. That is why, despite the relative brevity of the text, we have chosen to present our findings in book form. We are convinced that only a publication devoted solely to Fr Ffrench's unhappy experience with the Canadian Church can achieve that goal.

The Historical Significance of Fr Ffrench's Experience

Some readers will argue that Fr Ffrench is not an historical character of major importance and so does not merit such a detailed study. In some ways this assessment is understandable, in that Fr Ffrench was neither of high ecclesiastical rank nor incumbent in a position of power. When considered from such a perspective, Fr Ffrench was indeed a missionary among many. Nevertheless, the repercussions of his life and activities in North America were much more extensive than has been generally recognized. To be specific:

At the regional level, Fr Ffrench was actually a major influence in the early development of English Catholicism in Maritime Canada, and not just because of the large number of persons he converted. Even Archbishop Plessis (then Bishop Plessis) found himself obliged to point out to Fr Antoine Gagnon, who would one day become Vicar General and would be known as "the builder of churches," that Fr Ffrench had established more church structures in two years than had Fr Gagnon in twelve.[3] Historians seem to have forgotten Fr Ffrench's achievements in favour of perpetuating the scandal connected with the accusations against him.

At the national level, Fr Ffrench's case is, as far as we have been able to ascertain, the most glaring example of the negative results of French-Irish tensions in the early nineteenth-century Canadian Church. These tensions have barely begun to be probed by scholars. Fr Ffrench's case provides a clear illustration of how disastrous certain policies of the time turned out to be, and it may well turn out to be the most important chapter in this whole field of study.

At the international level, there is no doubt that Fr Ffrench's experience in Canada played a central role in complicating an already complex situation in New York. Without Archbishop Plessis' intervention and Fr Malou's aversion to Fr Ffrench, the story of trusteeism there would have been quite different. This case alone illustrates the extent to which internal Church policy within Canada, apparently affecting only one humble missionary

---

[3] AAQ RL IX no. 47, Plessis to Gagnon (Quebec, 11 Nov. 1816).

and one local incident, could have both long-range and long-term effects.

In other words, the significance of Fr Ffrench's case in Church history, in Canada as well as beyond our borders, has surely been under-estimated. Far from being a peripheral figure in events of importance, he was a key participant. This truth will almost certainly come to be acknowledged once the facts of his case are better known and his role can be objectively evaluated.

Sources and Methodology

The analysis and arguments in the following nine chapters rely principally on original documents and letters, some of which have been unavailable to earlier critics, or at least elusive. The best-known and most accessible documents are held in the Archives of the Archdiocese of Quebec and in the Archives of the Propaganda Fide in Rome. Still others have been unearthed in Boston, Baltimore, Lisbon and Dublin. The City of Saint John itself has furnished valuable material. Among the rarer documents located are those written or published by Fr Ffrench himself. Two of these are particularly valuable in that they bear directly upon the events on which some of the accusations against him were based.

These last, along with two other documents, comprise the four appendices. The first appendix is a defence, chiefly a compilation of documents written by others and collected by Fr Ffrench when he returned to New Brunswick in 1822 in an effort to counter allegations of immorality against him. It includes a recantation by a false witness, asserting also that she had just written to Archbishop Plessis informing him of her recantation; this witness' letter to the archbishop was ultimately ignored by its recipient.

The second appendix is essentially a biographical document, discovered in Rome. In it, Fr Ffrench relates how and why, as a child, he converted to Catholicism, subsequently travelled to Portugal for training as a Dominican, and finally became a missionary in the New World.

The third appendix consists of a petition to the pope for permission to found a Dominican college at Saint John. It was the favorable reply, by Pope Gregory XVI, to this document that Bishop Bernard Donald Macdonald chose to ignore when Fr Ffrench returned to New Brunswick for the last time in 1840.

The final appendix, while superficially the least interesting of the four, is significant in terms of Maritime church history, in that it represents a document implicitly offering Rome some suggestions as to how the region could be carved up to form a second vicariate apostolic. The actual placement of the boundaries of this hypothetical "second see," as it has been referred to by historians, was long a subject of speculation, and Fr Ffrench's analysis of the area, while not terribly interesting to the casual reader, sheds some light on this question.

Except for Fr Ffrench's will, which has been located, and his extant correspondence, to which the textual body of this book often refers, these are all the known surviving documents written or dictated by Fr Ffrench. It is therefore fitting that they be published appended to the study of which they form an integral part.

Unless otherwise indicated, all translations from French or Latin are our own.

As far as secondary sources are concerned, most critics of the past have been obliged to rely on hearsay or assumption when mentioning Fr Ffrench in the context of events in which he participated. We have, of course, reviewed their comments and their references, but so few of them have given Fr Ffrench the benefit of the doubt that they have scarcely been a factor in the preparation of this book. The major ones will be cited in chapter 9. One study in particular, however, deserves to be given special recognition. This is a lengthy unpublished manuscript by the late Victor O'Daniel O.P., entitled simply "Appendix E." It was originally intended to be part of a book on Fr Thomas Carbry, who was involved in events in the United States.[4] O'Daniel is one of the few historians to judge Ffrench innocent of the accusations made against him, and for this his remarks in earlier publications have been disparaged by more than one historian. We do not claim to agree either with all of O'Daniel's assertions or with all of his conclusions. His "Appendix E," however, has furnished us with more than one line of fruitful inquiry, as well as with an encouraging concurrence with some of our ideas, and we do indeed wish to acknowledge our debt to that worthy scholar. Given that the voices of Ffrench's detractors have been much more numerous and much more vociferous than those of his proponents, it is a pity that O'Daniel's "Appendix E," whatever its deficiencies, was never published, in some guise or other, during an earlier decade. If it had been, the arguments for Fr Ffrench's innocence might well have been investigated more closely, or at least taken more seriously, by scholars before now.

Organization of the Material

Because it is not possible to discuss any one phase or aspect of Fr Ffrench's case without a detailed knowledge of the sequence of events, a chronological presentation of those events, with accompanying analysis, will form the structure of the first seven chapters. The fact that these chapters constitute a partial biography is therefore incidental. Within these seven chapters, a further sub-division according to the geography of events comes naturally into play as well. Thus, chapter one deals with Fr Ffrench's life before coming to North America, including those of his activities in Ireland and Portugal having later repercussions in the New World; chapters two and three analyze his activities in Canada up to and including the events that led to his departure for the United States in 1818, as well as his

---

[4] This document is presently housed in the archives of the Dominican Province of Saint Joseph, Providence College, Providence, Rhode Island.

reaction to the charge of immorality; chapter four studies the nature of the opposition to his taking the bishop's side against trusteeism in New York, while chapter five deals with Rome's reaction to his activities there as well as to those of his opponents; chapter six analyzes the reasons for his failure to clear his name upon his return to New Brunswick in 1822; and chapter seven offers a look at pertinent events subsequent to his leaving that area in 1826. In other words, these seven chapters present a detailed description and analysis of events relating to the "case of Fr Charles Dominic Ffrench." Once these details are fully understood, the final two chapters become possible: chapter eight assesses the role of nationalism at the various steps, and chapter nine traces the role played by critics in prolonging and disseminating an inaccurate portrait of this little-known clerical figure.

By including the appendices as supplementary material and illustration of some of the arguments in the text, we express the hope that they will become a useful tool for future researchers. For one thing, copies of them have not been easily accessible elsewhere. Only one of them has ever been published, and that one by Fr Ffrench himself some one hundred and eighty years ago. By making accessible in one place the text of all these documents, while at the same time providing complete documentation on the case most centrally concerned with them, we hope to send a signal to scholars that further work in the area of ethnic or nationalistic tensions in the early Canadian Church would be a useful field of study. In other words, by choosing to present completely the case of one Irish missionary, we are suggesting that sustained research on some of the other apparently minor figures of the period might prove to be an abundant source of historical riches.

It would have been fitting that these chapters be completed by a photographic or artistic illustration of their subject. However, no portrait of Fr Ffrench has so far been found in any of his domicile countries.

View of Saint John, 1814, by Joseph Brown Comingo. Courtesy New Brunswick Museum, Saint John, N.B. (1966. 100A).

Chapter 1

FFRENCH'S EARLY YEARS: IRELAND AND PORTUGAL (1775-1812)

Charles Ffrench was one of five children born to a family belonging to the Anglican squirearchy of western Ireland.[1] His father Edmund, mayor of the town and the Protestant Warden of Galway, traced his lineage back several centuries to one of the thirteen Anglo-Norman settler families who, because of their wealth and education, ultimately rose to positions of power and influence. By Cromwellian times these families had come to be known as "the tribes of Galway." During the eighteenth century, a period of considerable religious instability in Ireland, two wardenships emerged. One was the official Protestant wardenship, which had originally been Catholic but had been taken over by the Established or Episcopal Church; it represented only a minority of the citizens and had little impact on the history of the town. The other, or effective, wardenship had the support and interest of the majority, who were Catholic. During the same period, several of the Ffrenches endeavoured to shore up and secure their precarious fortunes by renouncing the Catholic Church and crossing over to the Established Church.

---

[1] Unless otherwise indicated, material on Ffrench's early life is taken from his hand-written memoir, "The Conversion of Charles Ffrench to the Catholic Church" ["Conversion"], dated 26 April 1840 and presently housed in the Archives of San Clemente in Rome [SCAR]. The complete text of this document can be found in Appendix B. Pagination indicated in subsequent references to it is that of the original, not of the transcribed text. An excellent work on the Catholic Wardenship of Galway is that of Martin Coen, *The Wardenship of Galway* (Galway: Kenny's Bookshop & Art Gallery, 1984).

Charles' mother, Ann Ireland, was the daughter of an Episcopalian notable, whose roots were in the province of Connacht. Married at the age of fourteen, she died suddenly when she was twenty-one and young Charles still less than a year old. On her deathbed she became a Catholic, with Warden Edmund's acquiescence. Thomas, first Baron Ffrench and a cousin to Edmund, was a leading Catholic peer in the region.

Upon the death of Warden Ffrench in 1786, Charles and his nearest sibling, named Edmund after their father, were raised by a strict but generous grand-aunt who entrusted their education to a Protestant minister named Dr. Shaw. The latter, a kindly man, performed his duties so well that the young Charles thought him "at the very summit of perfection," later commenting, "It would appear that such attentions working on minds full of sensibility would form a strong barrier to our conversion."[2] In spite of Shaw's influence, two incidents of those early years exercised a deep and abiding influence on the boy. Already, at the age of four, Charles had secretly followed a servant girl to midnight mass and had been profoundly affected by the Catholic liturgical service, in particular by the solemnities surrounding the mass. Then, when he was fourteen, a second chance attendance reinforced the impressions of the first so much that the experience proved definitive. As Charles Ffrench himself put it, "Whatever prejudices that I enbibed from my friend Parson Shaw, seemed in a moment to lose their influence on my mind."[3] This change in the direction of Ffrench's spiritual life soon afterwards resulted in a successful effort to persuade his brother Edmund to take instruction with him in the Catholic faith.

When, after three years of covert study and debate, the two boys were publicly received into the Catholic Church, the response of their Protestant relatives was marked by threats,

---

[2] "Conversion," 12.

[3] "Conversion," 15. In quotations from the "Conversion" and other documents of the period, all idiosyncrasies of spelling and punctuation have been retained without comment, unless specific changes or corrections are signalled along with the reference.

cries, entreaties, and tears. Finally, their guardian, who was also their maternal uncle, offered them a choice: either they would enter Trinity College, Edmund for the church and Charles for the law, or all support would be withdrawn and they would be turned out as paupers into the streets. Upon their refusal their uncle was as good as his word, and for a while they were, as Charles put it, "reduced to the necessity of entering mercantile houses, to gain our subsistence."[4] Both had determined to enter the priesthood but, unfortunately for them, the times were inauspicious for young men seeking places in Catholic seminaries. Abroad, France was still in the throes of revolution and closed to such aspirants. At home, the Royal College of Maynooth (later St. Patrick's) was, by law of the trustees, inaccessible to the sons of Protestants. At this juncture, Edmund, who wished to become a Dominican and was perhaps inspired by the career of a distant Catholic relative, Peter Ffrench O.P., who spent 25 years on the Mexican mission,[5] induced Charles to make application with him to a priory of that Order at Esker, a short distance from Athenray.

Their applications were favourably received and they entered there as novices, both making their religious profession in 1795. They were then sent to do their theological study at the College of Corpo Santo in Lisbon, Portugal. There, on 23 December 1797, the two brothers received tonsure, minor orders and the subdiaconate at the hands of the Inquisitor General in the oratory of his palace at the Rocio. The following year, on 10 June 1798, Edmund received the diaconate from the bishop of Marianne, although Charles was not raised to the diaconate before another full fifteen months had elapsed, on 21 September 1799. In his "Conversion," the latter implies that the delay was related to health problems, possibly those that intermittently afflicted him later on in North America. Holy Orders were

---

[4] "Conversion," 20.
[5] *Dictionary of National Biography* VII, 693.

bestowed on both brothers by the Inquisitor General on 21 December 1799.[6]

Upon his return to Dublin in 1801, Charles settled upon two priorities for his ministry, namely, the conversion of his beloved grand-aunt and her Protestant relatives, and the organization of a private academy for boys of the upper classes. During these several years of his residence in Ireland a considerable success attended Ffrench's efforts in both ventures. As he had been appointed assistant pastor to a church near his academy, a good deal of his time was also taken up with parochial duties. Even so, his efforts attracted the notice of Archbishop John Thomas Troy, who, along with Dr. John Milner and other members of the Catholic hierarchy, encouraged him in his plans to establish an anti-veto gazette in Ireland. In furtherance of this project, Ffrench pledged all the personal property he had acquired. Unfortunately, the enterprise would eventually fail, and he would be forced to lay out large sums in order to satisfy its creditors.[7]

---

[6] VA ANL, Ms. 284 matriculas de anno 1793 ate 1797: 23 Dec. 1797; Ms. 290 matriculas de annos 1798, 1799, 1800: 10 June 1798, 21 Sept. 1799, 21 Dec. 1799.

[7] VA ANL vol. 26, fols. 186-187, Ffrench to Nuncio (Lisbon, 4 Jan. 1812). The anti-veto project was related to events leading up to the Catholic Emancipation Act of 1829. In an effort to further the cause of emancipation, some Catholic authorities at this period sought to make a conciliatory gesture to the government and specifically to accept that any appointment by Rome of a Catholic bishop should be subject to veto by the king. The veto act was never put into law.

Some readers may wonder why Ffrench, as a friar, would involve himself in commercial ventures, either in Dublin or later. However, such activity was not unusual at the time for Dominicans not living within the religious community. Indeed, many of those who became missionaries were at least partly supported by relatives or were obliged to turn their hand to money-making of some sort in order to survive. It will be noted that Ffrench's financial activities in Ireland were sanctioned by Archbishop Troy and that Bishop Plessis, despite his later antipathy towards the Dominican, at no time chastened him for involving himself in commercial affairs.

The experience of Ffrench's academy in Dublin also merits examination at this point. This school was opened in either 1806 or 1807. Boarding students (10) and day scholars (100) were both in attendance, the former paying 40 guineas each per year and the latter each subscribing a much lesser sum. Five instructors were employed to teach the fourteen subjects offered over the five years of study. Ffrench visited each class morning and evening, in order to examine the daily progress made and to enter it in the Judgement book with which each student was provided. This daily routine was settled upon in order to permit him to attend to his duties in the nearby parish. The school was a success, providing him with a comfortable living and an ample return. After paying expenses there was sufficient left over to offer a suitable pension to two widows, to provide education, books and stationery to eighteen orphans, and to educate, support and clothe two orphans living in his house, who, when suitably prepared, were to be apprenticed abroad.

During these satisfying years, Ffrench was also asked by a wealthy woman, whose husband was a drunkard, to take charge of her investments. This he did, placing one part of them with a well-respected and wealthy man, a Mr Lewis, who gave bond security for them, and the remainder with a confidential friend and proven broker, one Richard Coyne. Held in high esteem by the bishops of Ireland and the clergy of Dublin, Coyne was, by appointment, Bookseller to the Royal College of Maynooth.

By 1810, Ffrench had decided that the time had come to hand over the direction of his school to others, and to take up a suggestion made by his first convert, a Mr Taylor whom he had met in England while travelling home to Ireland from Portugal in 1801: namely, that he go on the American mission. Before crossing the Atlantic on his way to "the great western world," he decided to make a long detour via Lisbon, in order to pay his respects to an ailing relative there. Before sailing for Lisbon, Ffrench turned over to Coyne the administration of his school as well as his various assets, cash, bonds and debentures, the whole having a value of more than £1000. After Ffrench's departure for

Lisbon in 1810, Coyne appropriated increasingly large amounts from the trust for his own purposes and, by mismanagement and malfeasance, bankrupted the cleric's account. Also lost were the woman's debentures to the value of something under £1000.[8]

Ffrench's experiences of these three financial ventures are significant because they would bear upon later events in his life. In short, rumours about them would play a role in the Dominican's problems in the New World. For several years following this last incident Charles Ffrench would endeavour to find the means to repay the sum lost by the woman through Coyne's dishonesty. In addition, several spurious claimants, learning of his later acquisition of interests in New Brunswick, would attempt to seize control of them but would be frustrated by Edmund, who held powers of attorney. Fr Ffrench would one day write that his property in Saint John was so heavily mortgaged that he possessed only the name of it.[9]

Ffrench planned to stay no more than a month in Lisbon. As matters turned out, his sojourn in Portugal stretched to nearly two years. For the most part, the long delay was caused by the chaotic and unstable situation that the Portuguese kingdom was then enduring. In late August of 1810, a Napoleonic army under Marshal André Masséna initiated a major offensive against the Portuguese. The Duke of Wellington, who was leader of the defence forces, responded by ordering that the entire Portuguese countryside, from the national frontier to Lisbon, be laid waste. Thousands of country people fled to the hills and the seaports. Ships' carpenters worked night and day, fitting out vessels to carry the inhabitants' property to safety. Inside the capital, the royal family made preparations to flee to Brazil. All convents

---

[8] "Conversion," 25; VA ANL vol. 26, fols. 190-191, Edmund Ffrench to Charles Ffrench (Dublin, 5 Dec. 1811); AAB no. 32, Ffrench to Benedict Fenwick, Bishop of Boston (Portland, 10 May 1838). The ailing relative in Lisbon, a Madame Connolly, died while Ffrench was in Portugal and left large sums of money to charitable and religious groups, including the Dominican Order in Ireland.

[9] AAB no. 32, Ffrench to Fenwick (Portland, 10 May 1838).

and churches received instructions for securing their plate and other treasures. At Corpo Santo, the community devised a plan to sell off its two colleges, Corpo Santo and Santo Sucesso, in order to save their wealth for the mission. To make matters worse, all types of communication were interrupted by these events. Contact between the College of Corpo Santo in Portugal, the Dominican Provincial authorities in Ireland, the delegate of the Nuncio—the Nuncio himself had gone to Brazil with the royal family—and the Master General of the Order, who happened to be in Italy, all but broke down completely.[10]

In the midst of this confusion, the new rector for Corpo Santo, Nicholas Murphy, arrived from Dublin. Over the first eight months of his administration, Murphy proved to be entirely unsuitable for the office: he refused to wear his habit, he was refractory towards his seniors, and he was contemptuous of his subjects.[11] It was at this time that Ffrench, who was resident in the college during most of his time in Lisbon, received news that his school in Dublin had gone into bankruptcy and that its creditors were howling for compensation. He seems to have determined to return to Dublin in order to settle affairs there, but Edmund, who was already in Dublin, advised him that his presence was not necessary and offered to act as his agent, provided that Charles give him powers of attorney. Archbishop Troy, who was privy to the matter, seconded Edmund's proposal and recommended that Charles have the British minister at Lisbon affix his seal to the written instrument.[12]

---

[10] AAD 117/7, Francis Archer to Troy (Lisbon, 20 Sept. 1807); AAD 117/7, Vincenzo Macchi to Troy (Lisbon, 30 June 1811).

[11] AAD 117/7, Macchi to Troy (Lisbon, 12 Nov. 1810); AAD 117/7, Macchi to Troy (Lisbon, 30 June 1811).

[12] VA ANL vol. 26, fols. 190-191, Edmund Ffrench to Charles Ffrench (Dublin, 5 Dec. 1811); VA ANL vol. 26, fols. 188-189, Troy to Ffrench (Dublin, 23 Dec. 1811). Edmund Ffrench remained in Ireland, where he became Bishop of Kilmacduagh and Kilfenora in 1825.

While waiting to learn details of his school's failure, Ffrench was asked by Murphy to help out in the College school. After a time, however, the two men fell out. In a letter to the papal nuncio, Ffrench outlined his view of the situation: "Out of justice to the children, I saw that they needed other masters and [to] stop following a system which up till then served only to fill Mr Murphy's pockets." The new rector countered by representing Ffrench as "a thief forced to flee Ireland," and he denounced him to Vincenzo Macchi, the nuncio's delegate, as well as to anyone else who would listen. To the great displeasure of many, including the Archbishop and the Dominican Provincial of Ireland, he publicly expelled Charles from the College. In addition, Murphy wrote a derogatory article about the College of Corpo Santo in an Irish magazine, and this further inflamed feelings. Delegate Macchi summoned Murphy before him, asserting that the article was a calumny and that Murphy was obliged in conscience to withdraw it and to restore Ffrench's good name. In concert with another clergyman, Ffrench himself subsequently opened a school in competition with the College school.[13] Murphy's loose remarks and irresponsible writing would, however, cause lasting damage to Ffrench's reputation, for they would later be invoked against him when he became involved in controversies in America.

In the event, Murphy's mistreatment of Ffrench served to confirm the conviction of the nuncio's delegate, the Provincial, and the Archbishop, that the rector should be removed.[14] Indeed, Archbishop Troy even proposed to Macchi that Ffrench be

---

[13] VA ANL vol. 26, fols. 186-187, Ffrench to Nuncio (Lisbon, 4 Jan. 1812); VA ANL vol. 26, fols. 192-193, Edmund Ffrench to Charles Ffrench (Dublin, 15 Feb. 1812); AAD 117/7, Macchi to Troy (Lisbon, 28 March 1812); AAD 117/7, Macchi to Troy (Lisbon, 3 May 1812).

[14] AAD 117/7, Macchi to Troy (Lisbon, 30 June 1811; 28 March 1812; 18 July 1812); VA ANL vol. 26, fol. 184, Ffrench to Nuncio (Lisbon, 10 Jan. 1812); VA ANL vol. 26, fols. 192-193, Edmund Ffrench to Charles Ffrench (Dublin, 15 Feb. 1812).

appointed vicar *ad interim*. Macchi refused, on the reasonable grounds that Ffrench was too young and did not speak Portuguese; furthermore, although Macchi implied this rather than stated it directly, Ffrench was also considered unsuitable for the office by having cited Murphy before the civil courts for redress, which act was forbidden by canon law.[15]

Exceedingly disillusioned by the course that affairs were taking, and having the promise of a dimissory letter,[16] which he later received, from Fr Patrick Gibbins, the Provincial of Ireland, as well as letters of recommendation from Archbishop Troy, Ffrench determined to leave Portugal as soon as a ship was ready to depart for America. Thus, on 15 May 1812, he set sail and, after a voyage of two months, made landfall at Saint John, New Brunswick.[17]

While Charles Ffrench was in transit, the Dominican Provincial chapter met and recommended that he be promoted to the office of Preacher General of the Order. This event appears to reflect its recognition of his preaching and proselytising services in Ireland and Portugal, for, although still young, he had already been highly successful in both activities.[18] Indeed, it would be especially as a preacher and proselytiser that Ffrench would be valued by the religious public in the various missions he would one day serve in North America.

---

[15] AAD 117/7, Macchi to Troy (Lisbon, 28 March 1812); VA ANL vol. 26, fols. 180-181, Ffrench to Nuncio (Lisbon, 15 April 1812); AAD 117/7, Macchi to Troy (Lisbon, 3 May 1812).

[16] A dimissory letter to a priest gives its recipient permission to leave the diocese.

[17] "Conversion," 25-26; AAQ RL IV 14, Troy to Plessis and Gibbins to Plessis (Dublin, 27 and 28 Nov. 1812); AAQ RL VII 443, Plessis to Troy (Quebec, 3 Nov. 1812); VA ANL vol. 26, fols. 180-181, Ffrench to Nuncio (Lisbon, 15 April 1812).

[18] TA vol. 1, 9 July 1808 and 20 Jan. 1812; AAQ RL VII 443, Plessis to Troy (Quebec, 3 Nov. 1812).

Travelling on the River Saint John, 1817, by Emeric Essex Vidal. Courtesy New Brunswick Museum, Saint John, N.B. (W6798).

Chapter 2

A SMALL TASTE OF SUCCESS: QUEBEC AND NEW BRUNSWICK (1812-1816)

Ffrench intended to go to the United States, but hostilities between Britain and that country had broken out, and as a result American ports were closed to British shipping. Travel by land, both difficult and dangerous at the best of times, was impractical for similar reasons.[1] By a stroke of luck, however, word reached him in Saint John that Bishop Joseph-Octave Plessis of Quebec had just completed his second visitation to his Atlantic stations and was making his way back to the St. Lawrence by way of St. Basile in the Madawaska mission. Ffrench hastened up the Saint John River to intercept him, and, after his month-long stay as guest of Fr Louis Raby, the resident missionary at St. Basile, friar and bishop met on 7 September 1812.

Plessis readily accepted Ffrench's offer of service, on the understanding that he exercise his ministry as a curate in Quebec during the following year. Ffrench was advised to return to Fredericton, where he had stored his books and baggage, in order to supervise their transport to Quebec City personally.[2] By the end of September, the bishop and his new recruit, who would become known to most of his clerical colleagues in Canada as Père Dominique, had been reunited in Quebec. Ffrench was

---

[1] AAQ RL VII 443, Plessis to Troy (Quebec, 3 Nov. 1812); *New-Brunswick Courier* [Saint John], 1 Dec. 1827, quoting *St. Andrew's Herald*.

[2] "Conversion," 26; Msgr. J.-O. Plessis, *Journal de deux voyages apostoliques dans le Golfe Saint-Laurent et les provinces d'en bas, en 1811 et 1812* [*Journal de deux voyages*] (Quebec: Le Foyer Canadien, 1865), 271-275.

appointed a vicar and began to acquaint himself with the discipline of the diocese.[3] Over the following months he seems to have pursued a routine of preaching and proselytism among the Protestant elements of the population. In this enterprise he was so successful that he later wrote of it, "My bishop was constantly anoyed by the troublesome visits of the Protestant Bishop." He was not exaggerating. In point of fact, Jacob Mountain, the Anglican Bishop of Quebec, went so far as to propose that Ffrench be tried for high treason because of his missionary work among Anglicans![4]

Toward the end of April 1813, Ffrench was suddenly incapacitated by so severe a bout of what he termed stomach trouble that ten days passed before the risk entailed in moving him to hospital could be taken. His recovery was slow, and, if other seizures that he had of a similar nature may be used as a gauge, painful in the extreme.[5] At about the time of this illness, Plessis decided that Père Dominique would be sent to the Miramichi in July, provided, of course, that he had returned to good health by that date.[6] Missionary faculties were, in fact, formally accorded to him on the second of that month. His

---

[3] *Répertoire général du clergé canadien, par ordre chronologique depuis la fondation de la colonie jusqu'à nos jours*, ed. Cyprien Tanguay (Montreal: Eusèbe Senécal et fils, 1893), 175; *Liste chronologique des évêques et des prêtres, tant séculiers que réguliers, employés au service de l'Eglise du Canada depuis l'établissement de ce pays, et aussi la liste des évêques des autres possessions britanniques de l'Amérique du Nord*, ed. F.-X. Noiseux (Quebec: T. Cary, 1834), 37.

[4] "Conversion," 27. In April of 1813, Bishop Jacob Mountain wrote to Governor Sir George Prevost to ask that he punish Ffrench for having converted local Protestants. This, he contended, was a form of high treason and Ffrench's punishment would provide a salutary example for other Roman Catholic priests to respect the king's religion (Thomas R. Millman, "Mountain, Jacob," in *Dictionary of Canadian Biography* VI [1821-1835], 528).

[5] AAQ RL VIII no. 78, Plessis to Jean-Henri Roux, Vicar Apostolic of Montreal (Quebec, 11 May 1813).

[6] AAQ RL VIII no. 77, Plessis to Roux (Quebec, 4 May 1813).

instructions, which accompanied his commission, were fairly precise. He could work in all of the maritime settlements, including the Gaspé region, and the Îles de la Madeleine, but his main efforts were to be focused on the Miramichi district and its six stations, namely, Taboujemtèque (now Tabusintac); Saint Bernard's at Neguac; Saint Anne's at Burnt Church; Saint Peter's at Bartibog; Malcom's Chapel; and Saint Lawrence at Bay of Winds (now Bay du Vin). Each station was to be visited twice a year and for as long as was needed to instruct and catechise the people, both young and old.[7] Accompanied by the missionary at Richibucto, Antoine Gagnon, Ffrench left Quebec City for New Brunswick on 26 August 1813, arriving at Richibucto two weeks later. Before his departure from Quebec City, the Irish community there presented him with a handsome purse containing more than £81 and a testimonial signed by 62 persons, nearly half of whom he had personally converted to Catholicism.[8]

Apparently the two men, Ffrench and Gagnon, did not get along well, for disagreements developed at the beginning of the voyage and at its end. In his correspondence, Ffrench never mentions these clashes, nor does he express any particular dislike or criticism of Gagnon. The same cannot be said of his companion. At the time, Gagnon simply recorded that the reception given to Ffrench on the Miramichi was warm and welcoming, particularly on the part of the Protestants, who turned out in large numbers to hear him preach at the Sunday mass over which he presided.[9] It is clear from Gagnon's report of

---

[7] AAQ 124 Registre des insinuations ecclésiastiques, vol. H fols. 47r-48r, 2 July 1813, Pouvoirs extraordinaires accordés à Mr Charles French, Missionaire de Miramichi, Instructions données à Mr Charles French. The spelling of place names varies considerably in the correspondence of the period. Quotations that include any passage in which place names appear will adhere faithfully to the spelling used by the letter-writer; otherwise the modern spelling will be used.
[8] SCAR, Charles Ffrench dossier, doc. 1; "Conversion," 27.
[9] AAQ NB V no. 31, Gagnon to Plessis (Shediac, 8 Oct. 1813).

the trip, however, that he had taken a strong dislike to the Dominican, and this antipathy surfaced to colour almost all his remarks about Ffrench later on.

As Ffrench rapidly discovered, conditions in the mission were in a sorry state. The Catholic population, which consisted of Acadians, Irish, Mi'kmaq, and Scots, was not only relatively small, it was dispersed along the waterways and bays, beside such roads as existed, and in isolated hamlets in the outback. At Bartibog, the designated seat of the mission, the presbytery was virtually in ruins, scarcely adequate for shelter in summer and completely uninhabitable in winter. Despite the clergy's pleas and exhortations to make repairs, the congregation had so far responded only with promises. The other stations were in even more desperate straits, for even where there existed church and rectory, the buildings were so dilapidated as to be unfit for either worship or dwelling.[10] Even so, Ffrench set to with a will and, within three years and despite the harsh climate under which he suffered and the numerous obstacles thrown up by parishioners, he transformed his mission.[11] But the cost to him personally was great, for the effort seriously jeopardized his health. Old stomach disorders returned, while exposure to the cold, where the only relief to be found was in damp and draughty buildings, brought on a debilitating case of rheumatism.[12]

---

[10] AAQ NB VI no. 143, Ffrench to Plessis (Bartibog, 30 May 1815). For details about conditions and travel along the sea coast, as well as along the Miramichi Bay and River, see Joseph Gubbins, *New Brunswick Journals of 1811 & 1813*, ed. Howard Temperley (Fredericton: New Brunswick Heritage Publications, 1980), 74-85.

[11] "Conversion," 28; AAQ NB VI no. 147, Morisset to Plessis (Bartibog, 14 Oct. 1816); AAQ RL IX no. 41, Plessis to Ffrench (Quebec, 5 Nov. 1816); AAQ NB V no. 39, Gagnon to Plessis (Bouctouche, 15-16 Oct. 1816).

[12] AAQ NB VI no. 143, Ffrench to Plessis (Bartibog, 30 May 1815); "Conversion," 29-31; AAQ NB VI no. 145, Ffrench to Plessis (Bartibog, 14 Jan. 1816).

Ch. 2. A Small Taste of Success 37

Ffrench's principal consolation during these trying times was the success of his efforts at Saint John. His first visit to that city, after his arrival in the Miramichi mission, was in June 1814. Registry office records show that during the summer of that year he purchased three lots of land in the Horsfield-Charlotte Street block from William Durant, John Dean, and Thomas Horsfield. The following September, with the money he had been given by his Quebec admirers and the sale of his library, he acquired a further 630 acres, along with buildings and improvements, fronting on the Kennebecasis River at Norton.[13] Although no documentary proof of his presence in Saint John or in Norton at these times has been found, it is reasonable to assume that he was there, in order to arrange these transactions. According to local tradition, one confirmed by a writer of the last century, Ffrench began his pastoral activity among the City's Catholics with the celebration of mass in the courtroom of the old market building at the foot of King Street. Although the exact date of the mass is disputed, there is no doubt that this was the first service of its kind in the City, and the first in the region that was to become the County, since Fr Joseph Bourg's visit in 1779.[14]

Ffrench and the Saint John congregation seem to have taken to one another from the beginning. The Dominican reported to Bishop Plessis that Saint John was a small community, heavily

---

[13] VA ANL vol. 26, fols. 192-193, Valentine Bodkin to Ffrench (Galway, 15 Nov. 1812); Registry Office Saint John [ROSJ] 321 no. 2152, Thomas Horsfield to Ffrench (13 July 1814); ROSJ 323 no. 2153, William Durant to Ffrench (13 July 1814); ROSJ 325 no. 2154, John Dean to Ffrench (31 Aug. 1814); Registry Office Hampton [ROH] 347 no. 1814, Willis Knox to Ffrench (7 Sept. 1814); AAB no. 32, Ffrench to Fenwick (Portland, 10 May 1838).

[14] Pacifique de Valigny, O.F.M. Cap., *Chroniques des plus anciennes églises de l'Acadie* (Montreal: L'Echo de Saint-François, 1944), 58-59; Joseph Wilson Lawrence, *Footprints or Incidents in the Early History of New Brunswick* [*Footprints*] (Saint John: J. & A. McMillan, 1883), 85n. Lawrence places the incident in 1813 but that date is clearly at odds with Ffrench's own chronology. The year 1814 fits better the sequence of events.

influenced by Protestant practices, but one that quickly became, as he put it, "disposed litterally to follow my advice."[15] One of his first recommendations to the town's faithful was that they should have a chapel and, to that end and conforming with diocesan practice, a panel of five church wardens or trustees was set up. John Toole, a Loyalist victualler and sportsman, acted as treasurer of the group, while Bernard Kiernan, soon to be Deputy Surveyor-General of the province, assumed the role of secretary.[16] A building committee was then struck and a subscription opened, with Ffrench making appeals to both the Catholic and the Protestant residents of the town. By the last half of August 1814, £400 had been collected in Saint John and the same amount in Halifax, where Ffrench had also made a personal solicitation. These monies were given over to the wardens for the purchase of two lots of prime land on the then eastern edge of the City, where Sydney and Leinster streets now meet and where St. Malachy's High School presently stands.[17]

That autumn, volunteer labour cleared and prepared the site and laid down the foundations for a structure measuring 64 feet by 40 feet. Before leaving Saint John for the Miramichi in early September, Ffrench encouraged the congregation to assemble each Sunday for public prayer. Shortly after his return to Bartibog he received a letter from the Saint John Catholics asking that he present a memorial to Patrick Lambert, the Vicar Apostolic of Newfoundland, for assistance in their church-raising efforts. The building committee, it said, had come to the sad realization that much more money was required than the sum they had in hand. As for Ffrench, he was delighted to take up

---

[15] AAQ NB VI no. 143, Ffrench to Plessis (Bartibog, 30 May 1815).

[16] AAQ NB II no. 1, Saint John Catholics to Plessis, Nov. 1815; *Royal Gazette* [Saint John], 29 Aug. 1814; AAQ NB II no. 27, Philip Kehoe to Plessis (Saint John, 26 May 1821); Lawrence, *Footprints*, 85n.

[17] AAQ NB VI no. 143, Ffrench to Plessis (Bartibog, 30 May 1815); AAQ NE IV no. 95, Edmund Burke to Plessis (Halifax, 30 Aug. 1814); *Royal Gazette*, 29 Aug. 1814.

what he called a "glorious" enterprise and, after a quick visit to each of the Miramichi stations, he set off for Newfoundland in October 1814.[18] Although Ffrench intended to remain in Newfoundland only a month, the onset of winter and the cessation of the weekly sailings by packets travelling between Halifax and St. John's stranded him there. He turned the delay to advantage by preaching "charity sermons" in aid of the Saint John chapel and the Miramichi stations. As a result, when he returned to Saint John in the spring of 1815 he carried with him some £600. It would have been more, he wrote to Plessis, "were it not for the total failure of the fisheries of the preceding season." Of this amount, £420 was turned over to the Saint John building committee, the remainder being reserved for Malcom's chapel and the Bartibog church. At the end of March, work on the Saint John church was renewed when a contract for the delivery of building materials was let. Then, in mid-May, a call went out for tenders, to board and shingle the structure.[19] During the summer, while work was still going on, Bishop Plessis arrived on the scene.

This was the first ever recorded visit of a Catholic bishop to the City of Saint John. Plessis' diary recounts that he spent a few days in the City before proceeding up-river and another couple of days on his return, and that on both occasions he put up at John McKee's inn, an establishment he described as expensive but hospitable and decent. He estimated that within the City there was a Catholic population of fifteen families, observing wryly that the majority of them were as active and absorbed in the pursuit of temporal concerns as their Protestant fellow citizens. He was, nevertheless, impressed by the depth of their religious fervour and encouraged by the information that there

---

[18] AAQ NB VI no. 143, Ffrench to Plessis (Bartibog, 30 May 1815); AAQ NB VI no. 144, Ffrench to Plessis (Bartibog, 20 Oct. 1815).

[19] AAQ NB VI no. 143, Ffrench to Plessis (Bartibog, 30 May 1815); AAQ NB VI no. 144, Ffrench to Plessis (Bartibog, 20 Oct. 1815); *New-Brunswick Courier*, 28 March and 13 May 1815.

were many other Catholics in the district who concealed their faith out of anxiety for their civil rights. He was especially touched by the "heartbreaking" expressions they used in asking that a priest be assigned them. They were convinced, he wrote, that if one were sent, his presence alone would encourage those who were compelled to disguise their faith to be more open and courageous about their religion. Indeed, there was a good chance, he felt, that some "dissatisfied" Protestants would be drawn to the church if there was someone to preach to them and teach them the true faith.

Plessis' diary notes about the chapel under construction are cursory. It was, he remarked, like most other churches in the region, constructed of wood and but half-finished. He had been informed that an additional $1200 to $1400 would be needed to complete it, a portion of which, it was anticipated, could likely be obtained by a provincial grant during the coming session of the Legislature.[20]

The bishop's operational sentiments seem, however, to have been slightly at variance with those expressed in his diary. On his return to Saint John from Fredericton and the missions of the upper valley he wrote to Ffrench, who was now back in the Miramichi, castigating him for not keeping in touch with his superior as he was supposed to do, for having abandoned his mission for a lengthy period to go to Newfoundland, and for having the Saint John Catholics build a church "four times larger than their present population required." The congregation, too, came in for its share of criticism. Most of all, wrote Plessis, it had not assembled for Sunday prayers as it had been urged to do. Until he had been well informed that the parishioners were

---

[20] *Journal des visites pastorales de 1815 et 1816* [*Journal des visites pastorales*], ed. Henri Têtu (Quebec: Imprimerie Franciscaine Missionnaire, 1903), [1815] 111-113. Although currency is usually stated in pounds in the documents consulted, these particular figures are given in dollars.

assembling regularly, Ffrench was not to visit them again.[21] On Sunday, 27 August 1815, the day before his departure for Eastport and Boston, Plessis offered the first mass in the still unfinished chapel, formally placing it under the title and patronage of the primate Archbishop of Armagh, St. Malachy. In the course of the liturgy, he again enjoined his audience to meet regularly for prayers and, as a gesture of support for them, promised them the sum of £75 to assist in acquiring a cemetery.[22]

It is tenable to assign to that same autumn the second of Ffrench's known visits to Hampton, then the shire town of the region and located between Saint John and Norton. On 3 October he was, in all probability, in that village, for on that date he obtained from William and Polly Secord the deed for a further 160 acres of land, this time on the Pancake Creek near Norton.[23] Near the end of December, he was once more back in Saint John to preach a "charity sermon" so that the Congregation could finish the building, as funds for it were nearly exhausted. This event yielded an additional £30.[24] It is very likely in the interval between Plessis' departure and Ffrench's return to the City that

---

[21] AAQ RL VIII no. 450, Plessis to Ffrench (Saint John, 26 Aug. 1815). Ffrench had written to his bishop on 30 May 1815, but the letter did not arrive before Plessis' departure from Quebec City; the bishop's subsequent letter to Ffrench, dated six months after Ffrench's own, would state that it arrived in his absence (AAQ NB VI no. 143, Ffrench to Plessis [Bartibog, 30 May 1815]; AAQ RL VIII no. 516, Plessis to Ffrench [Quebec, 28 Nov. 1815]).

[22] *Journal des visites pastorales*, [1815] 132-134 and App. A, 179. In his *Tending the Flock: Bishop Joseph-Octave Plessis and Roman Catholics in Early 19th Century New Brunswick* [*Tending the Flock*] (Saint John: Diocese of Saint John, 1998), 185, John Jennings cites a figure of £25. However, we have retained the figure mentioned by Plessis himself in his journal.

[23] ROH 194 no. 2050, William and Polly Secord to Ffrench (3 Oct. 1815).

[24] NAC MG 23 Di vol. 61, Raymond Collection Notebooks, Series 1, no. 2; AAQ NB VI no. 144, Ffrench to Plessis (Bartibog, 20 Oct. 1815).

the two parishioners, Andy Sullivan, a tailor from Bandon, and John Flanagan, described by historian John F. Maguire, who wrote the first book on the Irish in North America, simply as "a college-bred man," convoked the congregation periodically for prayers, the reading of scripture, and a homily.[25]

In the meantime, Bishop Plessis, who was still in Boston, was negotiating for a former Newfoundland priest to take over the Saint John mission so that Ffrench could concentrate on the Miramichi area. In anticipation of a positive response, the bishop drew up two letters, the one to Ffrench and the other to the Saint John congregation. The first one released Ffrench from any further obligation to the people of St. Malachy's and limited his sphere of activity to the Miramichi valley. The other introduced Ffrench's prospective successor to prominent members of the Saint John congregation.[26] At about the same time, Plessis contacted Patrick Lambert, Vicar Apostolic of Newfoundland, requesting additional facts about the priest he was considering for Saint John, as well as information about a cleric he had met there, who had applied to work in the Quebec diocese. Ffrench's behaviour during his stay in Newfoundland seems also to have been on the prelate's mind, and his questions about him suggest the new direction his thoughts were taking. "Did he behave in an irreproachable manner?" Plessis asked Lambert. The latter being absent from the colony, it was the Vicar General, Thomas Ewer, who responded, negatively on the subject of the candidate for Saint John and positively for the applicant for work in Quebec. As for Ffrench, Ewer had "heard nothing of him, unworthy the

---

[25] John Francis Maguire, *The Irish in America* (London: Longman's, Green & Co., 1868; reprint: New York: Arno Press and the New York Times, 1969), 87-88. In October, Ffrench informed Plessis that his directive for the congregation to assemble for Sunday prayer had been complied with (AAQ NB VI no. 144, Ffrench to Plessis [Bartibog, 20 Oct. 1815]).

[26] AAQ RL VIII no. 453, Plessis to A. Fitzpatrick (Boston, 5 Sept. 1815); AAQ Reg. H fol. 107v, Plessis to the Inhabitants of Saint John (Boston, 15 Sept. 1815).

character of a clergyman." And Ewer had had ample opportunity to formulate an opinion, Ffrench having been his house guest for almost a month.[27]

That Plessis would ask such a question about Ffrench reinforces other indications that by the autumn of 1815 he had begun to entertain misgivings about the Dominican's service and suitability. His reservations appear to have had a dual origin, the one specific and direct, the other amorphous and circuitous. To the former category belong Ffrench's failure to keep his bishop abreast of affairs in his mission, his prolonged absence from it, and the apparent extravagance of the Saint John chapel. Not only did the reported size of the structure annoy the bishop but what he then believed to be Ffrench's role in its planning and construction vexed him as well.[28]

Another factor contributing to the bishop's upwelling ill humour was Ffrench's application to Protestants on both the Miramichi and Saint John rivers for financial aid to complete his building projects. The bishop's dislike of the practice was made abundantly clear in a letter he wrote to Ffrench in late November 1815. "The best route in these types of enterprises," he advised, "is to accept what the Protestants give without asking them for anything."[29] The philosophy inherent in such an approach, he defined later, in a letter to another missionary, William Fraser of Kingston. "The generosity of our Protestant brethren is indeed praiseworthy," he wrote, "but if considered *in rerum natura* their contributing to the building of Catholic chapels is nothing but a homage they pay to their lawful brethren they have abandoned without even the shadow of a right."[30]

---

[27] AAQ RL VIII no. 451, Plessis to Lambert (5 Sept. 1815); AAQ TN I no. 47, Ewer to Plessis (St. John's, Dec. 1815).
[28] *Journal des visites pastorales*, [1815] 113; AAQ RL VIII no. 393, Plessis to Pierre-Marie Mignault (Quebec, 2 Jan. 1815).
[29] AAQ RL VIII no. 516, Plessis to Ffrench (Quebec, 28 Nov. 1815).
[30] AAQ RL X no. 405, Plessis to Fraser (Quebec, 3 Sept. 1821).

Plessis was similarly uncomfortable about the facility with which Ffrench established himself in the esteem of prominent members of the Protestant community wherever he went.[31] "Do you know," he asked the Dominican, "that there are Protestants who speak evil of you and reproach you for vices of which apparently you are not guilty?"[32] On the question of his clergy frequenting Protestants, Plessis seems to have drawn a fine line, one apparently characterized by motive. Though unwilling to condone social intercourse with non-Catholics, the bishop exhibited no reluctance when it came to Ffrench's cultivating their friendship in order to further their conversion to the Church. Thus, for example, one finds him encouraging Ffrench to cultivate the acquaintance of Richard Simonds–scion of one of the founding families of the province and one of its wealthiest–whom he himself had met while travelling up the Miramichi River. "This good man," Plessis wrote, "appeared to me extremely reasonable on the subject of religion. It would not take much to bring him to Catholicism. Try to cultivate him and

---

[31] Even before Ffrench left Quebec City for his New Brunswick mission, Plessis was complaining that the Dominican did not handle the Protestants in a satisfactory way (AAQ RL VIII no. 77, Plessis to Roux [4 May, 1813]). His reluctance to permit much fraternization between Catholics and Protestants was greatly at odds with established practice in many parts of the Maritimes. For instance, Allan MacDonald writes that on Prince Edward Island the two groups were on the best of terms and that Bishop Angus MacEachern may even have performed Protestant marriages when no Protestant minister was available (Allan MacDonald, "Angus Bernard MacEachern, 1759-1835: His Ministry in the Maritime Provinces," in *Religion and Identity: The Experience of Irish and Scottish Catholics in Atlantic Canada* [*Religion and Identity*], eds. Terrence Murphy and Cyril J. Byrne [St. John's: Jesperson Press, 1987], 63).

[32] AAQ RL VIII no. 516, Plessis to Ffrench (Quebec, 28 Nov. 1815). We have found no indication in the correspondence as to the nature of the vices to which Plessis alludes, unless his reference is to the rumour mentioned in Gagnon's letter to him of 4-21 Aug. 1814, a rumour that Gagnon himself discounted (AAQ NB V no. 33).

pray to God to convert him to the true faith." Despite his previous successes in gaining new Catholics for his Church, Ffrench himself was not optimistic this time about his chances of success. "I believe him [Simonds] unprejudiced," he wrote in reply, "but worldly interest will keep him back."[33]

Plessis' growing uneasiness about Ffrench, at this time and later, appears to have been moulded at least in part by reports from Antoine Gagnon, the missionary at Richibucto. Of his voyage with Ffrench in August of 1813, Gagnon had written that Ffrench had bombarded him with "Protestant prejudices and antipathies," and had discoursed wildly about ecclesiastical discipline and the customs of the diocese.[34] And any mention of the church at Saint John seemed to elicit from Gagnon some acerbic comment about Ffrench. According to him, Ffrench's church was going to cost £4000. "What a mad idea! It could come only from the brain of a monk, drunk with the pleasure of seeing himself free of the bridle, far from his superiors," he wrote to his bishop.[35] Where such a large figure came from Gagnon did not disclose, but it was one that the bishop at first accepted and, in turn, relayed to Fr Pierre-Marie Mignault at Halifax.[36] Gagnon later lowered his estimate of the cost of the "basilica," as he came to call it, to £2000, though the structure,

---

[33] AAQ RL VIII no. 450, Plessis to Ffrench (Saint John, 26 Aug. 1815); AAQ NB VI no. 144, Ffrench to Plessis (Bartibog, 20 Oct. 1815). Some years later, the Simonds family would cede land for a burial ground but would require that Protestants also be allowed interment there (AAQ NB II no. 96, John Carroll to Archbishop Panet [Saint John, 18 Feb. 1829]; AAQ RL XIII no. 37, Panet to Carroll [Quebec, 6 April 1829]).

[34] AAQ NB V no. 31, Gagnon to Plessis (Quebec, 8 Oct. 1813).

[35] AAQ NB V no. 36, Gagnon to Plessis (Bouctouche, 13 Nov. 1814).

[36] AAQ RL VIII no. 393, Plessis to Mignault (Quebec, 2 Jan. 1815).

he said, would still be bigger than any of the three other churches in town.[37]

Unfortunately, the information that Plessis received from Gagnon about the chapel's dimensions was no more accurate than that he received about its construction costs. In fact, by the time Gagnon retailed the last bit of gossip about the chapel's magnitude, the bishop had been made well aware of its true size and had learned that it was the congregation, not Ffrench, who had made the final decision in the matter: the Saint John Catholics had simply over-ruled Ffrench's proposal for a more modest structure. Furthermore, the Catholics of Halifax, who had donated money for it, had supported the Saint John congregation's decision, for they had donated as liberally as they had on the understanding that the building would be larger than current needs required. The Haligonians' own experience had generated their recommendation, since the first chapel they had raised in Halifax had turned out to be not half large enough for them; as a result, they were now faced with the prospect of having to frame a new and larger church. For his part, Ffrench himself believed that any comparison of conditions at Halifax and Saint John was inappropriate. There was, he asserted, little likelihood that the parish at Saint John would increase as rapidly as that of Halifax, at least not in his lifetime. But his voice on the question had gone unheeded.[38]

As it turned out, both Plessis and Ffrench were underestimating the rate by which the Catholic population of Saint John would grow, for in less than ten years the "basilica" would be far too small for its congregation.[39]

Another issue that Gagnon made certain had the bishop's attention was Ffrench's failure always to wear the cassock. One of his informants had remarked that Ffrench had neither the air nor the manners of an ecclesiastic, and that he walked about the

---

[37] AAQ NB V no. 37, Gagnon to Plessis (Kouchibouguac, 19-23-24 Jan. 1815).
[38] AAQ NB VI no. 144, Ffrench to Plessis (Bartibog, 20 Oct. 1815).
[39] AAQ NB II no. 59, Ffrench to Plessis (Saint John, 2 Dec. 1824).

streets of Saint John with a little cane in his hand and his hat over one corner of his ear, "like a low-life."[40] This report drew more reproaches from Plessis, who wrote to Ffrench, "You must no longer hesitate to wear ecclesiastical attire in your mission, where no priest has ever appeared in any other costume." In his reply, Ffrench assured the prelate that the three *soutanes* that he had had made in Quebec as well as a fourth made in New Brunswick were all well worn from use in every corner of his mission except Saint John.[41] He offered no reason, however, for not wearing the cassock in Saint John, although one can speculate that his lay apparel may have been one of the factors contributing to his popularity with the Protestants.

In the summer of 1814, Gagnon had also informed Plessis that rumours were circulating about Ffrench at Bay du Vin because the Dominican had been so indiscreet as to go into certain houses there, houses that he, Gagnon, had warned him were unsuitable for an ecclesiastic. There, Ffrench had found himself in the company of young girls too often and too late in the evening; Gagnon reported that Ffrench had even played his violin for them in the presbytery itself. Gagnon confessed to being quite willing to give Ffrench the benefit of the doubt. He judged that Ffrench was ignorant, "as is usually the case," of

---

[40] AAQ NB V no. 37, Gagnon to Plessis (Kouchibouguac, 19-23-24 Jan. 1815). More than a year before, Plessis had already made a comment to Gagnon about Ffrench neglecting the cassock and thereby being a "badly educated ecclesiastic" (ADSJ no. 25, Plessis to Gagnon [Quebec, 6 Nov. 1813]). And, during his visit to Prince Edward Island in 1812, Plessis had previously noted with disapproval that Angus MacEachern did not wear religious dress while travelling in his mission; see Ronnie Gilles LeBlanc, "Antoine Gagnon and the Mitre: A Model of Relations Between *Canadien*, Scottish and Irish Clergy in the Early Maritime Church" ["Antoine Gagnon and the Mitre"], in *Religion and Identity*, 101.
[41] AAQ RL VIII no. 516, Plessis to Ffrench (Quebec, 28 Nov. 1815); AAQ NB VI no. 145, Ffrench to Plessis (Bartibog, 14 Jan. 1816); AAQ RL VIII no. 599, Plessis to Ffrench (Quebec, 27 Feb. 1816).

what people were thinking and saying about him. "I believe," he wrote, "that he has been unjustly accused but I think he has been imprudent in something." Gagnon's reticence to believe the rumours seems to owe its strength, and even its source, to an experience of his own some time before, when he himself had been accused of siring a child by an aboriginal woman. "Fortunately for me," he admitted to his bishop, he had been away for a while and the rumour had died down.[42]

In addition to his role of embellishing and circulating accounts of this nature, Gagnon also acted as a ready cipher and sounding board for the bishop's ruminations about Ffrench. In a letter of early January 1815 to Gagnon–Ffrench had not yet returned from Newfoundland–Plessis had commented to him that the Dominican was a sorry figure, whom he would much prefer to be in Lisbon or Dublin than in a mission of his diocese, and that he would "thank anybody who had enough influence on his [Ffrench's] mind to make him lose taste altogether for [the diocese]." Gagnon took him at his word and recounted to Ffrench what the bishop had said about him. "That stirred up his bile a bit," Gagnon reported mischievously. His justification for such a breach of discretion was, he explained to Plessis, "to make a deeper impression on [Ffrench's] mind." As for the bishop, his correspondence indicates that he came to regret not expressing himself with more reserve.[43]

As Plessis' regard for Ffrench waned, that of the congregation at Saint John increased proportionately. In November 1815, the Catholics in the City drew up a memorial to the bishop, in which they embodied two requests: one, that he permit Fr Ffrench to visit New York during the coming summer, in order to solicit contributions from their rich fellow Catholics and countrymen there so as to be able to finish St. Malachy's, and, two, that Ffrench be assigned to reside among them. "He

---

[42] AAQ NB V no. 33, Gagnon to Plessis (Shediac, 4-21 Aug. 1814).

[43] AAQ RL VIII no. 394, Plessis to Gagnon (Quebec, 2 Jan. 1815); AAQ NB V no. 38, Gagnon to Plessis (Bouctouche, 9-11 Feb. 1816); AAQ RL VIII no. 35-1, Plessis to Gagnon (Quebec, 16 March 1816).

would soon plant Catholicity in our City," the memorialists asserted. To make these proposals more acceptable, the signatories held out the assurance that Ffrench was much esteemed by people of every persuasion and that he had, by his manner of preaching, been able "to banish that Spirit of Prejudice & rancour that raged so long" in Saint John. At the same time, they conceded that the rents from pews would be insufficient to maintain him, but they proposed that, if the rents were combined with the weekly collections, an annual stipend of £100 might be raised. The document was signed by thirty heads of families and single males, as well as by Garrett Toole who signed for twenty others, presumably those who could not write.[44]

This plea arrived too late to have any influence on Plessis' decision to appoint someone other than Ffrench to the Saint John mission. The offer of St. Malachy's, made in September 1815 to a Newfoundland priest, had had to be withdrawn because of what appears to have been that cleric's tarnished record. However, in October, Fr Paul McQuade of Albany had arrived in Quebec seeking work in the diocese. When the formalities of his exeat[45] had been satisfied in New York by its new and recently-arrived bishop, John Connolly, Plessis had therefore taken McQuade on and offered him Saint John.[46] McQuade would reach there the following spring.

Meanwhile, on the Miramichi, Ffrench was enduring a horrible winter, one in which his health was brought to the edge of collapse. Periods of severe rheumatism, colds, aching jaws, recurring stomach ailments, and bowel attacks, all but paralyzed

---

[44] AAQ NB II no. 1, Saint John Catholics to Plessis (Saint John, Nov. 1815).

[45] An exeat is written permission from a bishop for a priest to leave the diocese in order to take up an appointment elsewhere.

[46] AAQ NB II no. 2, McQuade to Plessis (Montreal, 16 Feb. 1816); AAQ RL VIII no. 589, Plessis to Connolly (Quebec, 21 Feb. 1816); AAQ Registre des insinuations ecclésiastiques 12A vol. H 118r, Plessis to McQuade (Quebec, 28 March 1816).

him. A constant diet of fish combined with cold, draughty shelters added to his misery. Called out to attend a dying man some twenty miles distant one frosty night, he set out on his horse, following a snow-cloaked stream. When about half-way to their destination, he and his steed crashed through the ice. It was only after extraordinary effort that he was able to save himself and his mount. The result of this mishap left him so disabled that, for some time afterwards, he had to be carried, prone like a corpse, when called out to visit the sick and the dying. There being no medical assistance in the region, he was compelled to depend entirely upon his small medicine chest. Even this was of no value when he suffered his most severe attacks. By January of 1816, his constitution had become so weakened that he deemed it essential to give up his mission for the more moderate climes of the United States. He would, he promised Plessis, remain at his post until August in order for a replacement to be found and to oversee the latest improvements he had initiated at his various stations.[47]

Plessis' reply to Ffrench's request for an exeat is dated 27 February 1816. In it, he assured Ffrench that he was not indifferent to the latter's decision to leave the diocese but, he agreed, "your health reasons are unanswerable. Rheumatism and our climate are two enemies that cannot live together." The southern states, he advised, will always be better for those afflicted with so cruel an illness. The interval before Ffrench's estimated departure date would, he told him, allow time to find a successor who was acclimatized, and the exeat was being sent now, "not to speed your withdrawal to foreign parts," but rather because he, Plessis, expected to be in Upper Canada from May until August and would thus be unavailable later to comply with such a request. Plessis also told Ffrench that he had found a good Irish priest (McQuade) who, he hoped, would consent to go to the mission at Saint John, although, he commented, that little

---

[47] AAQ NB VI no. 145, Ffrench to Plessis (Bartibog, 14 Jan. 1816); "Conversion," 30-31.

congregation scarcely deserved a pastor. He advised the Dominican that a pastoral letter had been written to the congregation of Saint John and addressed to John Toole. He would have sent it to Ffrench himself, he wrote, but he feared that the latter would have finished his winter visit to the mission before the letter arrived.

The tone of this letter is completely cordial. Despite Plessis' disparaging remarks about Ffrench in his earlier correspondence with Gagnon and his occasional reproaches to Ffrench himself, he seems to have been sufficiently content with the Dominican at this point for his letter to contain no words of recrimination at all.[48]

The last sacramental act performed by Père Dominique at the Miramichi mission was the rehabilitation of a marriage on 24 August 1816 at Bartibog. He had been detained a month longer than anticipated. Indeed, August had been a busy month for Ffrench, for he had performed seven baptisms and six marriages at three different stations. Five of the six unions were solemnized at Burnt Church, the witnesses of which were the full congregation of Mi'kmaqs.[49] His journey to Saint John followed upon these last duties and was both painful and slow. Ffrench's rheumatism returned and made it difficult for him to walk. He had frequently to be carried, "no small load," he wrote to Plessis, "as I am (if I dont exceed it) your Lordships weight."[50] A few weeks later he received a note from Plessis telling him that Fr Joseph Morisset would succeed him as missionary on the Miramichi, and formally thanking him for the services he had rendered to the diocese.[51]

---

[48] AAQ Reg. H fol. 116r, Plessis to the Inhabitants of Saint John (Quebec, 26 Feb. 1816); AAQ RL VIII no. 599, Plessis to Ffrench (Quebec, 27 Feb. 1816).
[49] Bartibog Register, vol. 3 (1813-1823), 60-66.
[50] AAQ NB II no. 5, Ffrench to Plessis (Saint John, 19 Sept. 1816).
[51] AAQ RL VIII no. 690, Plessis to Ffrench (Quebec, 20 Sept. 1816).

On the state of his mission at the time, Ffrench advised the bishop that the stone church begun by the Mi'kmaqs at Burnt Church was nearly finished, for it required only a roof to be completely enclosed. At Bartibog he had purchased sufficient lime, oil, and paint to complete the preservation and coating of the new church's exterior; he had, as well, reserved to its account £100 of the monies gathered in Newfoundland. At Neguac a small presbytery was underway, while at Bay du Vin the presbytery was finished and the new church rapidly approaching completion.

Along with this report, Ffrench enclosed a deed and a money draft. The former was for twelve acres of land on which Malcom's Chapel stood and which he had obtained from "old Malcom" before he died. Because he could not get the monies required to execute this transaction from the parishioners, Ffrench had to pay it out of his own pocket, hoping to be reimbursed later. By turning over the deed and account to Plessis, he hoped to make the congregation more acceptable to the bishop, whose policy was that parishioners be made to conform to the usages of the Diocese; those usages, wrote Ffrench, "the people in general of Miramichi are much disposed to resist," especially the issue of church pew rentals. The money draft was for £34, half of which was for the bishop and accrued from the dispensatory account during Ffrench's three years in the mission, the remainder being the balance of his account for church ornaments, which he had purchased through the agency of the Quebec seminary. Ffrench concluded his report with a request that his faculties be extended over the coming winter because it was then too late in the year for him to travel in his condition. He anticipated that by spring his health might permit him to move to a more salubrious climate.[52]

Upon his arrival at Bartibog in the autumn of 1816, Morisset reported to his bishop that he found the place pleasant and his reception by the Scots of the district heartening.

---

[52] AAQ NB II no. 5, Ffrench to Plessis (Saint John, 19 Sept. 1816).

Everywhere he went he heard only good about Ffrench.⁵³ A few days after receiving Morisset's letter, Plessis received another, this time from Antoine Gagnon, the missionary at Richibucto. In contrast to his usually censorious remarks about Père Dominique, Gagnon's pronouncements on this occasion amounted to a veritable paean of praise. He reported that Ffrench had left the Miramichi in early September, having left his various churches more advanced than one could reasonably desire, given the few means at his disposal. "The monks have very special talents to succeed where others always fail," he declared. "So, where no missionary has succeeded in having a chapel at Bay of Winds shingled completely he has found the means to do so, to have his presbytery expanded and to have a beautiful church in the course of completion." But there was even better. Ffrench had succeeded in animating the parishioners there and in giving them a will that they did not have before except when the missionary was present. In speaking of the Dominican's illnesses during the winter of 1815-1816 and the following summer, Gagnon displayed in his letter an unexpected degree of compassion. His epistle ended with the remark that he had told more about Ffrench to the bishop than was necessary.⁵⁴ But his generous sentiments on this occasion went unrewarded. In reply, Plessis tweaked Gagnon with the remark that the Dominican had built more structures in two years than had Gagnon in twelve, that Ffrench had, in fact, retired with honour.⁵⁵

On 5 November 1816, Plessis granted the extension of faculties requested by Ffrench, saying, "I authorize you to preach and to hear confessions, even to give absolution in reserved

---

⁵³ AAQ NB VI no. 147, Morisset to Plessis (Bartibog, 14 Oct. 1816).
⁵⁴ AAQ NB V no. 39, Gagnon to Plessis (Bouctouche, 15-16 Oct. 1816).
⁵⁵ AAQ RL IX no. 47, Plessis to Gagnon (Quebec, 11 Nov. 1816). For a full account of Gagnon's career, see LeBlanc, "Antoine Gagnon and the Mitre," 98-113.

cases in all this province until revocation. As for the other functions, such as the celebration of marriages, the abjuration of the new converts etc., it is better that they be reserved for the pastors of the [various] places."[56]

Thus it was that Fr Charles Dominic Ffrench completed his first four years in North America. As the autumn of 1816 drew on, he convalesced in Saint John, awaiting the advent of springtime, when both personal and climatory circumstances would be more advantageous for his removal to the United States. In the meantime he assisted in the parish as much as his physical condition allowed, unaware that the month of April would bring, not an easement of his difficulties, but even worse trials than he had anticipated.

---

[56] AAQ RL IX no. 41, Plessis to Ffrench (Quebec, 5 Nov. 1816).

Chapter 3

TRIALS AND SETBACKS: NEW BRUNSWICK (1816-1818))

As these events were unfolding, the parishioners of Saint Malachy's received a response to their memorial. They were notified that the bishop was unable to assent to their request, Fr Ffrench having asked to be dismissed from the diocese in order to go to the United States. Furthermore, by the time this response reached Saint John, the bishop had already arranged that Fr Paul McQuade would go to St. Malachy's as the first resident pastor. A few days after receiving his commission, McQuade, in the company of the missionary to Madawaska, Fr Louis Marcoux, was on his way to New Brunswick. When the two men arrived at St. Basile in the spring of 1816 they found the Saint John River still iced over. McQuade therefore stayed with his companion until the ice broke up, so that he could travel on the river when it was again possible.[1] The result was that he did not appear in the City much before the third week of May. He performed his first sacramental duty, a baptism, there on 6 June 1816.[2]

At the end of October McQuade made his first report to the bishop. He had, he said, been busily engaged in making several

---

[1] AAQ NB II no. 2, McQuade to Plessis (Montreal, 16 Feb. 1816); AAQ Reg. H fol. 116r, Plessis to the Inhabitants of Saint John (Quebec, 26 Feb. 1816); AAQ RL VIII no. 624, Plessis to Marcoux (Quebec, 26 March 1816); AAQ NB II no. 3, McQuade to Plessis (Madawaska, 23 April 1816).

[2] ADSJ. Copies from original register held in AAB. McQuade took the earliest baptismal and marriage records with him when he left Saint John for Salem, Massachusetts, and it was only in recent years that the Saint John Diocese acquired a copy of them.

changes and modifications to the interior ornamentation and arrangements of the church: the altar had been reduced in size and "built in a semi-circle stile," while a tabernacle and thirty-two pews had been installed, and six candlesticks put in place. The expense entailed by these works appears to have contributed to much tension among, and alienation of, some members of the congregation. McQuade complained, "After paying the expences of the improvements, my expectation of being supported is but miserable as the congregation do not come forward to pay even what they have subscribed for." From the outset, John Toole, the treasurer-warden, made himself the chief spokesman for the resistance. When called upon to deliver up the church accounts and the monies gathered for church expenses, he had refused outright, offering no explanation for his conduct.[3]

One would not be far off the mark in attributing Toole's hostility to two factors, the first of which was the rebuff he and his fellow memorialists had received in their plea for Ffrench's appointment. Their immediate response to the bishop's decision, while couched in polite, even formal, terms, had betrayed a depth of feeling that was clearly much more than simple disappointment.[4] Secondly, it is more than probable that McQuade's imperviousness to criticism and advice, a failing that would be censured by Plessis a few months later, was being given full rein during the renovations undertaken at St. Malachy's. Either he failed to consult the congregation about the work he proposed to undertake or he chose to ignore and override its opinions and wishes. After his failure to get along with Toole, McQuade approached the secretary-warden, Bernard Kiernan, with the idea of arranging church business in the presence of Toole and John Sinnot. Again he was repulsed, and this time in "very improper language": in point of fact, he was threatened with physical violence. Fr Louis Marcoux, who was in Saint John on a visit, let it be known that he would refuse to

---

[3] AAQ NB II no. 6, McQuade to Plessis (Saint John, 30 Oct. 1816).
[4] AAQ NB II no. 4, John Toole to Plessis (Saint John, 25 April 1816).

Ch. 3. Trials and Setbacks 57

officiate at St. Malachy's if Kiernan were present without having apologized. This notwithstanding, Kiernan appeared for mass. He was ordered to leave but defied the challenge and, in the end, was forcibly escorted from the church.[5]

Affairs continued to deteriorate. It is clear that, by the beginning of 1817, McQuade had begun to believe, though wrongly, that the dissidents were being counselled and abetted by Ffrench. That suspicion prompted him to enquire of the bishop the exact extent of the Dominican's faculties, as well as his status in the mission. He reported that Ffrench was very popular with the Kiernan faction, especially with Toole. He also seemed disturbed that Ffrench did not visit him when in the City and had not informed him about the private activities of the malcontents.[6]

The bishop's response was short and certainly sharper than McQuade had anticipated. Ffrench, McQuade was told, had been given licence only to preach and hear confessions until such time as his faculties were revoked. Part of the bishop's note was actually curt. "I am no friend," he wrote, "to those quarrels of a pastor with his flock." How was it, he asked, that one such as Kiernan, who enjoyed a good reputation and had been deemed one of the heads of the Catholic congregation eighteen months before, should so quickly be regarded as "nasty and hostile"?[7]

A few weeks later, McQuade suffered another upbraiding from his bishop. Several reports from Saint John had reached Plessis, which, if taken at face value, placed the blame for McQuade's troubles with the congregation, as also some that had occurred earlier in Albany, squarely on McQuade's own shoulders. The charges against him included a disregard of the

---

[5] AAQ NB II no. 8, McQuade to Plessis (Saint John, 10 Jan. 1817); AAQ RL IX no. 110, Plessis to McQuade (Quebec, 12 Feb. 1817); AAQ NB II no. 10a, Toole et al. to Plessis (Saint John, Feb. 1817).

[6] AAQ NB II no. 8, McQuade to Plessis (Saint John, 10 Jan. 1817); AAQ NB II no. 9, McQuade to Plessis (Saint John, 4 Feb. 1817).

[7] AAQ RL IX no. 110, Plessis to McQuade (Quebec, 12 Feb. 1817).

rights of the church wardens by his assuming control over the pew rents and Sunday collections, and an excessive pursuit of his private concerns, such as the establishment of an elegant household crowded with relatives and adherents, to the detriment of the spiritual needs of his flock. Furthermore, Plessis told him, those who sided with him in the troubles were "not the most respectable" of the congregation. As for Fr Ffrench, Plessis voiced the suggestion that, considering the very high regard in which he was held by the congregation, his continued proximity alone may have unintentionally contributed to the discontent. To assist in the restoration of peace, the bishop enclosed a pastoral letter, which he ordered to be read to the parishioners.[8] Almost simultaneously, however, a letter from McQuade was on the way to the archbishop assuring him that the more effervescent spirits at St. Malachy's had quietened down.[9]

The prelate's earlier uneasiness about Ffrench returned and his unhappiness with developments at Saint John reached a crisis point in the spring of 1817 when he received a letter from Fr Morisset, Ffrench's replacement at Bartibog. "Until now," Morisset reported, "I heard only good things about Mr French. But yesterday I heard a horrible piece of news about him. A young girl of honest and respectable family gave birth to a child last Sunday, which she affirms under oath to be Mr Ffrench's and it looks just like him. The parents overcome with grief and resentment have given it widespread publicity."[10]

Plessis' reaction was immediate and inexplicable. Without initiating an investigation into the rumours, he despatched to Ffrench, on 15 June 1817 via McQuade, a revocation of his faculties to preach and administer the sacraments throughout the

---

[8] AAQ RL IX no. 137, Plessis to McQuade (Quebec, 9 April 1817); AAQ Reg. H fol. 154r, Plessis to the Inhabitants of Saint John (Quebec, 9 April 1817).
[9] AAQ NB II no. 11, McQuade to Plessis (Saint John, 16 April 1817).
[10] AAQ NB VI no. 149, Morisset to Plessis (Miramichi, 17 April 1817).

Diocese of Quebec. The complete text of the message reads as follows:

> Sir: From the moment that this letter reaches you, you will please abstain from the ministry, from preaching, and from the administration of the sacraments in all the extent of the Diocese of Quebec, given that we are revoking for causes known to us, all the powers that we have given you since you left the mission of St. Peter's at Bartabog, Miramichi River.[11]

Ffrench's response, which bears the date of 21 July, is one of unreserved submission, resignation and acceptance:

> I bow with profound submission and resignation to the sentence communicated by Your Lordships letter dated 15th ultimo. I shall endeavour to console myself with the hope that on an investigation of my conduct, the imputations (as yet unknown to me) will clearly appear without foundation. It adds no small affliction to find that the public are in possession of the contents of your letter. Some go so far as to say they read it. It would be ungenerous in me to suppose that Revd. Mr. McQuade would act so incautiously as to show it. Indeed he assured me he did not show it to any person, neither did he know what were the charges against me, and moreover that he would give me his oath that he never stated any to yr. Lordship. I told him his simple word was fully sufficient, that, if I gave cause of complaint I should think he should first warn me of it and this he never did. Let it be as it will, my character must suffer. But God's holy will be accomplished, and may he in his mercy forgive those who wish to injure me. May I implore that your Lordship will be so good as to let me know what am I accused of? I am sensible of the pain it must give yr.

---

[11] AABalt case 22a P1, Plessis to Ffrench (Quebec, 15 June 1817), copy verified by Bishop Panet.

> Lordship to feel oblidged to write that letter, and I am equally certain [of] the satisfaction, if not to say the joy it would give you to be assured of my innocence. Mr McQuade told me I could not say mass. I will refrain until I hear from your Lordship, tho such a prohibition dont appear to me to be contained in yr. letter.[12]

Plessis replied on 26 August, in even stronger terms:

> Sir, the powers that you have received since your discharge from the mission of Bartabog, being by their nature revocable *ad nutum*, I do not at all believe myself obliged to give an account of the reasons that I had for revoking them. It is not acceptable to me that you exercise [powers] any further in my diocese, and that is all. It needs virtuous priests who edify the church and not libertines who dishonour it. By examining your conscience, it will be easy for you to recognize that you have completed at Miramichi what you had begun at Quebec, and of which I was informed too late. Otherwise you would never have had the honour of being appointed to the ranks of my missionaries.
> In revoking your powers, I have not forbidden you to celebrate mass. But if you do yourself justice you will abstain from doing so of your own accord, until by a long and severe penance you have expiated faults equally dishonouring for a priest and for a religious.
> I pray God to have pity on your soul and am in the bitterness of my heart etc.[13]

Plessis never again wrote to Ffrench directly, addressing any further messages to him only through correspondence with others. Nor is there any evidence that he investigated the

---

[12] AAQ NB II no. 13, Ffrench to Plessis (Saint John, 21 July 1817).
[13] AAQ RL IX no. 201, Plessis to Ffrench (Quebec, 26 Aug. 1817).

rumours, any more than had Fr Morisset. Yet virtually every sentence of this, his last letter to Ffrench, assumes the Dominican's guilt.

During the remainder of 1817 and the first days of 1818 Ffrench was in residence at his Norton farm. From there he occasionally visited Saint John in order to transact personal business and to call on his friends. According to McQuade, Ffrench adhered faithfully to the bishop's prohibitions during this time and neither preached nor administered the sacraments. In fact, commented McQuade, "his mercantile pursuits seem to engross his whole attention."[14] Even so, rumours continued to circulate. In late October 1817, Fr Marcoux, the missionary at Madawaska, reported to the bishop that he had heard that Ffrench was at Kennebecasis with Toole's daughter and that it was widely held among the English and the natives that he had married her.[15] Although that rumour had no foundation in fact and appears not to have been resuscitated later in New York, Marcoux's report impelled Plessis to ask him to visit Kennebecasis and Passamaquoddy, so that he would be in "a position to give me more exact information about the two Irish priests." Although unnamed, the two clerics alluded to here were, without any doubt, Ffrench and McQuade. The closing remarks of Plessis' letter to Marcoux seem to confirm this point: "I have little confidence in either, much less in the older of the two. The excesses of the one and the miserliness of the other are equally apt to dishonour religion." The bishop ended his assessment with the caution that "one must not judge them before they are convicted."[16] That remark should be borne in mind in the light of later events, for that Bishop Plessis himself did not at any time follow this precept in the matter remains to this day one of the most striking aspects of the whole affair.

---

[14] AAQ NB II no. 22, McQuade to Plessis (Saint John, 4 Dec. 1817).
[15] AAQ NB IV no. 67, Marcoux to Plessis (Madawaska, 22 Oct. 1817).
[16] AAQ RL IX no. 304, Plessis to Marcoux (Quebec, 17 Nov. 1817).

No response to Plessis' order to Marcoux has been turned up in the episcopal correspondence. On 7 March 1818, McQuade informed Plessis that Ffrench had left for the United States, "on account, it is said, of embarrassed circumstances." He added, significantly, "[Ffrench's] departure has made rather an unpleasant impression upon the Public mind."[17] The unpleasant impression referred to here was not, however, a reaction to Ffrench's behaviour, but instead chiefly to the Saint John congregation's failure to have Père Dominique named pastor, and its disappointment was compounded, in no small degree, by frustrations arising from its ongoing squabbles with the incumbent, Fr McQuade.

While all this was going on, McQuade, too, came to the conclusion that there was no future for him in Saint John. According to his account, the parishioners refused either to honour his undertakings or to support him. In fact, he complained, "some weeks . . . I have not four shillings to depend upon." To make ends meet he was obliged to run up large debts in the City, from which practice, he fully acknowledged, he was relieved only through the intervention of Fr Jean-Mandé Sigogne, the missionary at Meteghan, across the Bay of Fundy. The same good Samaritan also furnished McQuade with an allowance to defray the cost of his daily necessities. In order to discharge his obligations to Sigogne, McQuade was obliged to send his nephew home to Ireland to solicit the requisite sums from family and friends. Given his prospects at St. Malachy's, he felt compelled to ask for an exeat, although he promised, at the same time, to remain in his post for three months or until his nephew returned.[18]

The alacrity with which Plessis complied with McQuade's request leaves little doubt that he wanted to be rid of him. The dimissory was issued in early July 1818 and hand-delivered by the Vicar Apostolic of Nova Scotia, Edmund Burke, later the

---

[17] AAQ NB II no. 17, McQuade to Plessis (Saint John, 7 March 1818).

[18] AAQ NB II no. 21, McQuade to Plessis (Saint John, 7 May 1818).

same month. By the middle of November, McQuade had left Saint John for Boston, where he took up service under Bishop Jean-Louis de Cheverus in the mission at Salem, Massachusetts.[19] In the interim, Plessis had written to Morisset at Bartibog suggesting that, instead of wintering with one of his colleagues, he spend some weeks, even months, in the City of Saint John.[20] Whether Morisset accomodated that wish cannot be confirmed. The tenor of his correspondence seems to imply that he did not.

St. Malachy's would remain without a priest for nearly three years. Contact would be sporadic between Plessis, the congregation, and Ffrench, who had reached New York in January 1818. In 1821, the archbishop would respond to an appeal from the congregation. Neither the appeal nor its reply have survived, which fact constrains one to deduce their contents from remarks made in later correspondence. Plessis would then offer to send Fr Morisset to St. Malachy's provided that Morisset be given £300 per annum for his services. The congregation would propose instead that it give him £200 and provide him with a rectory, its letter adding that, if for any reason Fr Morisset was unable to come, then the congregation at large fervently hoped that Fr Ffrench would be appointed to the church.[21]

It is clear that, notwithstanding the rumours reported by Fr Morisset to Bishop Plessis, Fr Ffrench was still very popular in Saint John and that the congregation of St. Malachy's would,

---

[19] AAQ RL IX no. 423, Plessis to McQuade (Quebec, 7 July 1818); Louis S. Walsh, *Origin of the Catholic Church in Salem* (Boston: Cashman, Keating & Co., 1890), 22; Robert H. Lord, John E. Sexton and Edward T. Harrington, *History of the Archdiocese of Boston, in the Various Stages of its Development, 1604 to 1943* [*Archdiocese of Boston*], 3 vols. (New York: Sheed & Ward, 1944), vol. 1, 701.

[20] AAQ RL IX no. 464, Plessis to Morisset (Quebec, 11 Sept. 1818).

[21] AAQ Reg. H fol. 265v, Plessis to the Catholics of Saint John (Quebec, 30 Nov. 1820); AAQ NB II no. 27, Philip Kehoe to Plessis (Saint John, 26 May 1821); AAQ RL X no. 278, Plessis to the Committee of Saint John Catholics (Quebec, 5 June 1821).

even three years after his departure, prefer him to Fr Morisset or any other priest. As for Ffrench himself, however, he at no time during this period made any request that the congregation's desire for his incumbency be granted. It would not be until 1822 that he would direct his thoughts to a possible return to missionary activity in New Brunswick, and then it would be principally in order to support himself while investigating the source and the exact nature of the old, now even more damaging, rumours that had cast such a shadow on his final months in that region.

Chapter 4

TROUBLES WITH TRUSTEEISM: NEW YORK (1818-1820)

After arriving in New York in January of 1818, Ffrench applied to Bishop John Connolly, a fellow Dominican, for faculties. This request the prelate readily and graciously granted on 22 January. Ffrench was subsequently posted to the church of Old Saint Peter's on Barclay Street, where he officiated along with the Belgian Jesuit, Pierre Malou.[1] In that city's milder and more salutary climate, and prospering from the warm welcome he received from friends, his health improved rapidly. Then, late the following summer, with the permission, and probably the encouragement, of Bishop Connolly, he accompanied Virgil Barbour, a young Jesuit scholastic, to Claremont in western New Hampshire, to visit Barbour's father, Daniel, a pastor and the most prominent ecclesiastical figure in the region. During the week he stayed with Daniel Barbour, Ffrench converted to Catholicism several members of the family and some of their friends. Daniel Barbour himself became a Catholic a few months later. These were the first fruits of what would prove to be one of the most fecund sources of religious vocations in the early American church.[2]

---

[1] Victor O'Daniel, *The Dominican Province of Saint Joseph* (New York: National Headquarters of the Holy Name Society, 1942), 151; James R. Bayley, *A Brief Sketch of the Early History of the Catholic Church on the Island of New York* (New York: New York Catholic Publication Society, 1870), 90.

[2] Daniel Barbour, *The History of My Own Times* (Washington, 1828), 19-20; Lord, Sexton and Harrington, *Archdiocese of Boston*, vol. 1, 740-752.

By the time Ffrench returned to his station, the storm clouds of "trusteeism" had already broken over New York. More than two years before, on 24 September 1815, the city's second church, dedicated to St. Patrick, had been formally opened, to service the burgeoning number of Catholics there. The church had been nine years under construction and had spawned a monumental debt, which, in the view of the newly-arrived bishop, the joint board of trustees was either incapable of or averse to managing. Incoming revenues were insufficient to meet even the salaries of the bishop and his clergy, let alone pay off the debt.[3] In the face of a looming financial disaster, Bishop Connolly had quashed the joint board of trustees and established a new and separate board for each church, one third of whose members were to be elected annually.

These changes had evoked a strident and fierce opposition on the part of the old wardens, their friends, and their supporters. Among them were Don Thomas Stoughton, the Spanish consul and one of those most responsible for establishing Catholicism in New York, Andrew Morris, the wealthiest member of the Catholic community in both City and State, and his son-in-law, Lewis Willcocks, a wealthy manufacturer.[4] Frs Pierre Malou and William Taylor encouraged, supported and advised this group, and promoted contact with the francophile element of the congregation as well as the French bishops in the United States. As for Connolly, his foremost supporters were Francis Cooper, the first Catholic to be elected to the State Legislature, the vast majority of the faithful, and most of the clergy, prominent among whom were Frs Thomas Carbry, Michael O'Gorman, and finally Charles Ffrench. A struggle then ensued for control of the two boards. At the first elections of the separate boards, in March 1818, the bishop was able to secure a panel favourable to his

---

[3] Peter Guilday, "Trusteeism," *Historical Records and Studies* 18 (March 1928), 49.

[4] Patrick J. Dignan, *A History of the Legal Incorporation of Catholic Church Property in the United States (1784-1932)* [*Legal Incorporation*] (New York: P.J. Kenedy & Sons, 1935), 98-99.

views at St. Patrick's but the old wardens prevailed at St. Peter's, Fr Malou claiming that he himself had been largely responsible for the latter victory.⁵ During the run-up to the next elections, that is, during the months preceding March 1819, the two priests at St. Peter's, Ffrench and Malou, emerged as the respective champions of the bishop's party and of its opposition, the old wardens. Both men campaigned ceaselessly, Ffrench exploiting to the full his renowned oratorical skills in the pulpits of the two churches, as also at meetings of the congregations, and at gatherings in tavern halls.⁶

Nor was campaigning restrained; indeed, behavioural excesses did no credit to either side. Finding himself out of favour with his bishop, Malou went so far, in April 1818, as to circulate widely a remarkable twenty-seven-page document entitled "Sincere exposé to serve for the justification of the conduct Of Father Pierre Malou Priest of the Society of Jesus aged 65 years in a critical situation in which he has found himself And of the decision on which depended peace and good order."⁷ For his part, Ffrench took it upon himself to publish a

---

⁵ AAQ EU IV no. 18, Malou to Plessis (New York, 9 Dec. 1818); Dignan, *Legal Incorporation*, 96-99. John Farley writes that, on election day 1818, four police constables had to be summoned to maintain order (*History of St. Patrick's Cathedral* [New York: Society for the Propagation of the Faith, 1908], 76).

⁶ AAQ EU IV no. 22, Malou to Plessis (New York, 21 May 1819); AAQ EU IV no. 24, Malou to Plessis (New York, 15 Nov. 1819); AABalt file no. 14, Connolly to Ambrose Maréchal, Archbishop of Baltimore (New York, 30 Dec. 1819).

⁷ AABalt case 22 F1. Among the recipients of this document, which was dated 20 April 1818, was the Vicar Apostolic of Montreal, Jean-Henri Roux, who was in no way involved in the controversy. In it, Malou wrote that he had been unjustly chastised by Connolly for having circulated material without his bishop's permission, but he defended himself in the following terms: "Can I be prevented, in my capacity as an American citizen, as a member of its congregation, as the oldest of its priests, from expressing an opinion that my conscience tells me is true and that it is my duty to declare?"

fiery two-page commentary on the issues being contested, addressing it to the members of the Roman Catholic Communion of the City of New York; in the document, he specifically identified as his adversaries Fr Malou, Mr Morris, and Mr Willcocks.[8] Malou, in turn, counselled Fr William Taylor, who, it was widely held, sought only the mitre. He also circulated hundreds of copies of a handbill bearing the names of those candidates opposed to the bishop, candidates who, he proclaimed, should be supported.[9] In addition, he wrote letters characterizing Connolly as weak and indecisive, in fact, as the gullible puppet of others. Some of Malou's letters were directed to Ambrose Maréchal, Archbishop of Baltimore, and some to Bishop Plessis.[10] Despite the occasional rebuff, Malou found willing listeners in both prelates, for both were French-speaking and both seemed to take his word for it that the Dominican was anti-French. To Plessis and Maréchal, Malou commented at length on Charles Ffrench and on the direction events were taking in the New York church. His letters, which are remarkable for their passionate outpouring of personal animus against Ffrench, were to do the latter irremediable harm.

Malou's first letter to Plessis on the subject, a long closely-written epistle, was dated 9 Dec. 1818 and bore the title "Complaints against the Rev. M. French formerly of the Diocese of Quebec." It began with an apology that a "simple priest" like himself should involve himself in matters that were not his business. However, Malou quickly excused himself by saying that, given the deplorable state in which the New York Church

---

[8] Georgetown University Archives, Charles Ffrench to the Members of the Roman Catholic Communion of the City of New York (n.d. [1819]).
[9] APF SOCG vol. 925, fols. 448r-455v, Connolly to Plessis (New York, 10 March 1820).
[10] For example, see AAQ EU IV no. 19, Malou to Plessis (New York, 15 Jan. 1819). Malou had likely met Bishop Plessis during the latter's visit to New York in 1815 (Plessis, *Journal des visites pastorales*, 160-162).

found itself, it was necessary that Plessis be informed, because Bishop Connolly was timid, fearful and weak. And, although Connolly's differences with the trustees had begun long before Ffrench's arrival, Malou claimed that trouble had really begun at Old Saint Peter's with Ffrench's arrival the preceding January.

Malou's initial complaints against Ffrench were quite personal. The first issue, he told Plessis, had concerned the lodging provided for the two priests, the trustees having offered a house that could suitably accomodate only one person. Although Malou and Ffrench had both shared that conclusion, only the latter had insisted on larger quarters and, against the advice of the old board of trustees, had rented other accomodations for 1 May 1818. When Ffrench's arrangements were sanctioned by the new trustees, a palpable rift had developed in the congregation. Malou claimed that his break with Ffrench had nevertheless really arisen from the friar's conduct and assumption of authority at Old Saint Peter's, an authority that was so intolerable that he, Malou, had been obliged to leave the rectory and seek residence elsewhere. He wrote Plessis that Ffrench preached very little, heard few confessions, and spent his time making visits from house to house, returning late at night, having drunk "red and white wine, brandy, gin, indeed anything he was given, without it ever showing." Expressing doubt that Ffrench had ever been as sick as he said he had, since he now looked very fit, and accusing him of being too interested in money as well as of having spoken out against the French priests and bishops, Malou wrote that Ffrench had publicly asserted that, by reason of his seniority in the priesthood, the management of both the house and the church was his.

To what extent these allegations were true it is now impossible to establish. Certainly, the two men did not get along and did take separate lodgings. There is no doubt, also, that Ffrench campaigned in taverns and private houses, especially among the Irish. That he over-indulged in alcohol, as Malou seems to suggest here, appears problematic, however, since

Malou admits that any such over-indulgence took place "without it ever showing," and since he himself had assuredly not been present to judge of it at the time. As for Malou's assertion that Ffrench had probably never been as sick as he said he had, there is no doubt whatever that Ffrench had been a very sick man indeed during the months before he left New Brunswick. These allegations were, however, of trifling importance in the larger picture.

Unfortunately for Ffrench, Malou also listed, in his long litany of complaints to Plessis, rumours of immorality on the part of the Dominican at his previous stations, rumours that Malou himself had been told were already circulating in Quebec and New Brunswick. Malou's letter to Plessis ended with a plea that the Quebec prelate either confirm or deny the rumours. It is to Malou's credit that he did not actually confine his request to a confirmation of the rumours, but that he allowed for the possibility that the bishop might deny them. On the other hand, his correspondence makes it clear that he fully believed them himself, and that he looked upon them as useful ammunition in his efforts to rid himself of a man he now considered his archenemy. His own aim in writing, Malou insisted to Plessis, was to prevent scandal by using the facts to force Connolly to send Ffrench away, or else, he added, "I myself will tell the priest to leave."[11] As it later became clear, a major player in bringing the

---

[11] AAQ EU IV no. 18, Malou to Plessis (New York, 9 Dec. 1818). In some ways, Pierre Malou's involvement in the New York struggle might be viewed as the inevitable result of his years in Belgium, where he was known as a political and revolutionary activist: he had been a leader in the Belgian insurrection against Austrian, and later French, domination of that country. Malou was therefore fully accustomed to playing an active role in events about which he felt strongly. He would later become involved in the controversies surrounding the appointment of bishops in the United States; for example, see his letter of 6 April 1825 to Propaganda (APF SOCG-SP vols. 935-948 [1825-1833], fols. 97r-98v). For an account of Malou's turbulent life, see Patrick J. Dignan, "Peter Anthony Malou, Patriot and Priest (1753-1827)" ["Peter

stories to New York, and so ultimately in their promulgation there, was a Canadian, Fr Jean Louis Beaubien of the Diocese of Quebec, who had visited New York for some weeks in the autumn of 1818.[12]

Despite the fact that Ffrench was in disfavour with Plessis, the latter's reaction was stern and unequivocal: "I know what should be thought of Mr F. and I will willingly let your bishop know what he himself ought to think of him whenever it pleases him to ask me about the matter."[13] Rebuked, Malou endeavoured to explain away his gross presumption in a second letter, even claiming that Ffrench had spoken out against the Jesuits, but Plessis did not rise to the bait.[14] The bishop may have been antipathetic towards Ffrench, but he was not about to be dictated to by a mere missionary priest from another diocese.

In the meantime, however, Malou was already trying another tactic, for he urged Lewis Willcocks to summon a special meeting of the two boards of trustees and place before the assembled members a list of the charges circulating against Ffrench, as well as Plessis' letter of reply. The ostensible purpose of the gathering was to squelch the rumours if Ffrench was deemed innocent or to send him away if they were true. To that end, Bishop Connolly, who was present at the meeting, was asked to write to Bishop Plessis and to inform the church wardens of Plessis' reply. But Connolly, too, refused to cooperate, giving two reasons for his rejection of the proposal:

Anthony Malou"], *Records of the American Catholic Historical Society of Philadelphia* 42: 4 (Dec. 1931), 305-343 and 43: 1 (March 1932), 62-96.

[12] AAQ RL IX no. 498, Plessis to Roux (Quebec, 24 Oct. 1818); AAQ RL IX no. 533, Plessis to Roux (Quebec, 7 Dec. 1818). For a summary of the circumstances surrounding this visit, see Laval Laurent O.F.M., *Québec et l'Eglise aux Etats-Unis sous Mgr Briand et Mgr Plessis* [*Québec et l'Eglise*] (Montreal: Librairie St. François, 1945), 162-163.

[13] AAQ RL IX no. 547, Plessis to Malou (Quebec, 2 Jan. 1819).

[14] AAQ EU IV no. 19, Malou to Plessis (New York, 15 Jan. 1819).

first, the church wardens had no right to interfere in a spiritual matter, and, second, Fr Ffrench had received a legitimate exeat from Bishop Plessis.[15]

The clique also adopted another ploy. Willcocks invoked his own friendship with the Bishop of Quebec in the hope of obtaining the same sort of response that Malou had sought. In his letter to Plessis, he mentioned precisely two charges: that of immorality and that of financial dishonesty, and he asked Plessis to make specific comments on either one or both of these accusations. Instead, Willcocks, too, was admonished, Plessis bluntly telling him that laymen were not the judges of the faith and conduct of a priest. On the other hand, Plessis stated flatly, "I have nothing to write to him [Ffrench], nor any certificate to give him that he can use to his advantage." Curiously enough, Plessis did not even see fit to clear Ffrench of the charge of financial dishonesty, which he knew very well was false. He also assured Willcocks that, as a church warden, he was free to pursue an investigation into the truth or falsity of the rumours about the accused person.[16] Whether the latter qualification can be interpreted as a partial reversal of Plessis' own concomitant statement is open to debate. Certainly, Victor O'Daniel has categorized it as such. In his unpublished manuscript, he comments: "It is left to the reader to judge whether or not this was an outright interference in the affairs of another diocese, an incentive to strife, and even an encouragement of schism. A howl would have gone up to heaven, had Connolly written in this wise to a layman in Quebec."[17]

---

[15] AAQ EU IV no. 20, Ffrench to Plessis (New York, 1 March 1819); AAQ EU IV 22, Malou to Plessis (New York, 21 May 1819); Leo R. Ryan, *Old St. Peter's: The Mother Church of Catholic New York (1785-1935)* [*Old St. Peter's*] (New York: United States Catholic Historical Society, 1935), 145.

[16] AAQ EU IV no. 21, Willcocks to Plessis (New York, 3 March 1819); AAQ RL IX no. 591, Plessis to Willcocks (Quebec, 25 March 1819).

[17] O'Daniel, "Appendix E," 163.

Ch. 4. Troubles with Trusteeism 73

Although dismayed by Plessis' refusal to provide some sort of written confirmation of Ffrench's guilt, Willcocks journeyed to Quebec, hoping to moderate the prelate's stand on the matter, but to no avail.[18] According to Laval Laurent, he then despatched a letter to an unidentified party in Saint John, but apparently received no response.[19] On the strength of later events, one possible contact may have been Richard Toole, of whom more will be said later.[20] Malou, too, tried to confirm the charges against Ffrench in Saint John, but had no more luck than did Willcocks.[21]

But what were, precisely, the accusations against Ffrench, apart from Malou's complaints about Ffrench's high-handedness and their personal relations?

The most damaging rumour circulated was that, while in the Miramichi mission, he had sired a child with a parishioner of honest and respectable family. It had, of course, been Morisset, Ffrench's successor, who had been the first to notify Plessis of this gossip, in April 1817,[22] and it had been his letter that had provoked Plessis' real wrath against Ffrench. One would have expected that, given the high esteem in which Ffrench was held in all quarters of the mission, Morisset would have undertaken a quiet investigation of his own, gathering as much information as discretion, time and tact permitted. Had he done so, he might have been in a better position to verify or refute the accusations at the outset. At the very least he might have garnered data

---

[18] Attempts to establish the precise time of Willcocks' visit to Quebec have not been successful. Reference to this visit is mentioned in AAQ EU IV no. 24, Malou to Plessis (New York, 15 Nov. 1819); in that letter, Malou claimed that Willcocks had "learned verbally" from Monseigneur Panet that the charges were all true.

[19] Laurent, *Québec et l'Eglise*, 165.

[20] See AAQ NB II no. 36, Mary Toole to Plessis (Saint John, 6 June 1822).

[21] AAQ EU IV no. 23, Malou to Plessis (New York, 23 June 1819).

[22] AAQ NB VI no. 149, Morisset to Plessis (Miramichi, 17 April 1817).

sufficient to enable him to advise the bishop that a good deal of insight and circumspection was needed in handling the matter. Unfortunately, neither Morisset nor Plessis, in his turn, had taken any such action.

Associated with the initial rumour were others of a sexual nature, including a report that Ffrench had been so imprudent as to visit the beds of women in the middle of the night, and another that he had debauched two sisters, who had perhaps even followed him to New York.[23] In addition, a Canadian priest, Fr Louis Raby, would formally depose to the Vatican that Ffrench had "wanted to seduce" his housekeeper several years earlier.[24] That there was no real evidence for any of these rumours seemed not to matter, and, as we shall see, Ffrench himself was eventually able to refute the principal ones, though not in time to save his reputation in New York. Unfortunately for him, the absence of proof did not prevent them from circulating freely.

Accusations were also made that Ffrench had mis-handled church monies in Saint John,[25] though all of the evidence indicates that, on the contrary, he had always been punctilious in the matter of monies entrusted to his care. It will be recalled that, on his return from Newfoundland, he had reported to Quebec the amounts and dispositions of the sums he had collected and that Plessis had subsequently approved of his arrangements.[26]

---

[23] AAQ EU IV no. 18, Malou to Plessis (New York, 9 Dec. 1818).

[24] APF Acta vol. 184, fols. 466r-471r, Guiseppe Mazzetti O. Carm., Consultor to Propaganda (Rome, 16 July 1820), 1, 5. Herein referred to as the Voto. Trans. Angelo Gualtieri. Pagination indicated in references to this document is that of the original, not that of the translation.

[25] AAQ EU IV no. 18, Malou to Plessis (New York, 9 Dec. 1818).

[26] AAQ NB VI no. 143, Ffrench to Plessis (Bartibog, 30 May 1815); AAQ RL VIII no. 516, Plessis to Ffrench (28 Nov. 1815). Ffrench also published an audit of parish finances in the local paper before he left Saint John, no doubt much like the one he would one day publish in the *Eastern Argus* [Eastport, Maine] of 6 Oct. 1838. Although Ffrench's *A Short Memoir* (see Appendix A) refers to such publication in the *City Gazette* of 19 Feb. 1817, this document cannot be verified because the *Gazette* of that date is missing from the New Brunswick Museum

Ch. 4. Troubles with Trusteeism 75

Furthermore, the congregation in Saint John had been so pleased by what the Dominican had achieved for it financially that it had memorialized Plessis for his consent to permit Ffrench to go to New York "in the hopes of finding among our fellow Catholicks & Countrymen Friends, who will readily come forward and chearfuly assist us" to complete the new church.[27] In addition, Ffrench's final letter to Plessis as missionary on the Miramichi had been as much a financial report as a pastoral review.

Charges against Ffrench's conduct in Lisbon and Dublin, and in particular the accusation that he had left Ireland because of the many debts he had accumulated there, had also been raised and relayed to Plessis by Malou.[28] Although there was never the slightest suggestion in Ireland that Ffrench had ever acted fiscally in other than a completely open and honorable way, it is true that his ventures there had ultimately turned out badly. Indeed, it will be recalled that Nicholas Murphy, the rector of Corpo Santo, had accused him of being "a thief forced to flee Ireland," and had been ordered to apologize to Ffrench. It seems likely, therefore, that events in Dublin had given rise to, or at least provided the seed for, these later rumours of fraud and thievery in Lisbon and North America.

That it was Fr Jean Louis Beaubien's visit to New York that had initiated, or at least amplified, all these rumours there, seems certain. When Ffrench finally did write to Plessis asking for some sort of denial of them in early March 1819, he brought up the subject. His long letter begins as follows:

> My lord:–I cannot omit the favourable opportunity
> which presents itself of addressing your Lordship, by

Archives in Saint John. According to Ffrench's own account, he appointed a committee to inspect the chapel accounts during the whole time of his administration. See also AAQ RL IX no. 41, Plessis to Ffrench (Quebec, 5 Nov. 1816).

[27] AAQ NB II no. 1, Saint John Catholics to Plessis (Saint John, Nov. 1815).

[28] AAQ EU IV no. 22, Malou to Plessis (New York, 21 May 1819).

Mr. Cannon, and at the same time of putting you in possession of matters regarding myself, since my arrival in this City, and which may be interesting to you. During my residence here, by irreproachable conduct, and strict adherence to the duties of the ministry, I have acquired the esteem of my most worthy Bishop, and the veneration of the Congregation.
The success of my labours did not confine itself to this City alone, but [has] been extended to the New England states, where, with God's assistance, I have brought over to our holy religion Revd. Mr. Barber, who was Pastor nearly forty years in New Hamshire, together with the principal part of his Congregation. Thus I was passing my days in happiness and utility to mankind, extending the house-hold of the Lord, rich in the estimation of the world, and I hope of God enjoying true peace and tranquility of mind; until that *unlucky* and *unpropitious moment*, which brought Revd. Mr Baubien to disturb it.
Little did I suppose when, for the sake of *truth*, I gave up every endearing prospect in this life, relinquished the friendship of my family, encurred their *enmity*, to embrace [the] Catholic Religion, that I would find in the very bosom of *that Church*, to which I clinged to in spite of every endeavouring opposition. A *most relentless enemy in the person of a Priest! a Brother!* Among the many assertions, which Mr. B. advanced, he affirmed that I robbed the *Cath. Church of St. John, N.B.* and carried off the funds to this country. Revd. Mr. Malou published this to all his friends. At length he gets Mr. Lewis Wilcocks to summon the two boards of Trustees of St. Peter and St. Patrick Churches, and the said Wilcocks arrains me of the *above scandalous charges* founded on the testimonies of Mr. B. & Mr. M., and on documents which the said Mr. Malou said he had from the hands of his Lordship, the Bishop of Quebec. You can easily conceive, my Lord, how much astonished must have been my Bishop, Doct. Connolly, at such

accusations, and more so being the first intimation he received of them.

There is no doubt that, given the already agitated state of politics at Old Saint Peter's Church, Ffrench was somewhat overstating here the "peace and tranquility" of his own life in New York before Beaubien's arrival. His account continued with a description of Willcock's intervention and the use of Plessis' reply to the latter as confirmation of the attacks against him; Ffrench concluded that, because these events did not at all confirm the gossip, the plans hatched against him by Malou and Willcocks had miscarried. In fact, Willcocks was bringing Ffrench before a lay court, and, in doing so, was liable to an action at law for defamation of character. Ffrench commented wryly, "If vague rumours and unfounded reports could constitute legal guilt, I would be condemned where I have worked out a painful & laborious Mission." Indeed, Ffrench was already so exasperated and irritated by Willcocks' actions and statements that, as the only way to obtain a respite from them, he brought a suit against Willcocks for $10,000 that same spring; Willcocks would then be obliged to defend himself against the charge of rumour-mongering.[29] Though this action on Ffrench's part might be understandable under the circumstances, it was not a move destined to meet with approval from the ecclesiastical hierarchy, especially as it was the second time in his career that he had initiated such a process.

Many accounts of this case have assumed Willcocks to be the victor, but to do so is to interpret events inaccurately. Unfortunately, as Patrick Dignan observes, "It would seem that even the Archbishop of Baltimore over-emphasized the value of the court decision against Ffrench, when he wrote to Propaganda on September 18, 1819: 'The scandal of the actions of Ffrench is such, that only seven weeks ago, he was brought before a court

---

[29] AAQ EU IV no. 20, Ffrench to Plessis (New York, 1 March 1819); AAQ EU IV no. 21, Willcocks to Plessis (New York, 3 March 1819).

of justice and condemned.'"[30] In fact, the results of the case itself might best be described as a draw. It was made clear that Ffrench had launched the suit only after Willcocks had refused to revoke the rumours, and that he had intended it to be the means of re-establishing his reputation. Ffrench therefore considered the result satisfactory in that it succeeded in doing so, at least partly. The proceedings brought out the fact that Willcocks had received all of his initial "information" from Fr Malou and that, although not summoned to court, Malou had in fact come there with Bishop Plessis' letter in hand, which letter, although not offering proof of Ffrench's innocence, by no means offered proof of Ffrench's guilt either, when it was read to the court. The case also publicized the fact that Bishop Connolly testified in court to Ffrench's integrity, considering him "innocent, not only of this charge but of every other, both before and after." On the other hand, Willcocks was not required to pay anything to Ffrench and was not convicted of circulating malicious rumours. He escaped condemnation because it was ruled that the trustees "were a body, at least as competent as any other to investigate the matter in the first instance: that the decision of a non suit, on that ground, was a positive justification of the plaintiff's character." Such, after all, was what the plaintiff, Ffrench, wanted most to establish. Journalistic reportage of the case was extensive, filling ten columns of *The Columbian* of 30 July 1819.[31]

But Charles Ffrench's troubles in New York were not over yet.

---

[30] Dignan, "Peter Anthony Malou," 73.
[31] *The Columbian* [New York], 30 July 1819. The *Columbian*'s report opened with the statement that a previous account of the case, published in the *Evening Post* and copied by other newspapers, had been neither unbiased nor complete, and that the *Columbian*'s "correct report" was for the purpose of "obviating the errors" published by others.

Chapter 5

ROMA LOCUTA EST, CAUSA FINITA EST: NEW YORK (1820-1822)

An appeal of the trustee elections of March 1819, formulated by Fr Malou and some of the former wardens, was carried to Rome by Fr William Taylor without his bishop's permission.[1] Taylor would spend many months away, returning only after the assessment to the plea had been delivered. During those months, letters and attestations aplenty would flow towards the Vatican, both in support of and in opposition to his position. In fact, Malou and the six disaffected trustees of St. Peter's continued to pour their complaints, charges, and censures into Baltimore and Rome. Archbishop Maréchal would side with Taylor, Malou, and the rebellious trustees, whereas Connolly would, of course, defend his own authority and his protection of Ffrench.[2]

The tempo of campaigning for the April 1820 elections speeded up as the voting date approached. Election day itself was marked with stormy scenes. At the end of the day, the door-to-door appeals made by Ffrench and O'Gorman had vindicated the bishop's position. Both Boards of Trustees were now filled with members who supported the principle that the powers of trustees were real but limited by canon law.

---

[1] According to Patrick Dignan, Taylor sought and got approval for this step from Archbishop Maréchal, who advised him to acquaint Connolly with his intentions, but when Taylor did so Connolly refused him permission ("Peter Anthony Malou," 77).

[2] AAQ EU IV no. 22, Malou to Plessis (New York, 21 May 1819); AAQ EU IV 24, Malou to Plessis (New York, 15 Nov. 1819).

At about this same time, Archbishop Plessis, as he was now, was on a visit to Rome, where Cardinal Francesco Fontana, Prefect of Propaganda, asked him to travel through and report on certain dioceses of the United States on his way home to Quebec. His visit to New York was brief, for he apparently arrived there on 21 July 1820, was already in Montreal by 7 August, and was back at his desk in Quebec City a month later composing his report to Fontana.[3] In addition, his examination of the situation in New York must have been cursory, and his discussions with those involved in the disputes less than ample, for his report was a virtual compendium of almost all the arguments already used by Connolly's opponents and Ffrench's enemies. In other words, it asserted that Connolly was a man estimable for his learning and for many virtues worthy of the episcopate, but blinded by Carbry and Ffrench, the latter of whom he, Plessis, had deprived of his powers in the diocese because of immorality. "Time has revealed against him [Ffrench] very dishonourable things of which the news has spread as far as New York," wrote Plessis in his report of 6 September to Cardinal Fontana, adding that, this notwithstanding, Connolly "continues to prefer him to the rest of his clergy ... and eases his mind with the knowledge that he has the support of the greatest number. But this great number is comprised of the Irish rabble that Ffrench knows how to incite and attach to himself, an ignorant and wild populace always ready to take sides, without thinking, for whoever succeeds in flattering them. The respectable Catholics ... confuse, in their discontent, their bishop with his protégé, speak of this prelate with little respect and finally split away from him." Plessis ended his account with the recommendation that, if Propaganda did not

---

[3] Jean-Baptiste-Antoine Ferland, *Mgr. Joseph-Octave Plessis: évêque de Québec* (Quebec: L. Brousseau, 1878), 223s. In a letter to the Prefect of Propaganda, Malou later wrote, of Plessis' visit to New York: "He arrived here, and after 36 hours he left for Baltimore, from where he returned two days later; after another stay of 24 hours, he left for Quebec" (APF SOCG-SP vols. 935-948 [1825-1833], fols. 114r-115v [New York, 14 Feb. 1825]).

see fit to appoint an Apostolic Commissioner to settle the issues, it became necessary for it to give the Bishop of New York an order to send Ffrench and Malou away. He admitted, albeit belatedly, that the latter, "finding himself at the head of the party opposed to Dr. Connolly, fans the flames and maintains the schism by very indiscreet and indecent words against a Bishop who sins only from having let his eyes be dazzled and who is inappropriately stubborn at not opening them to belief."[4]

The plea that Fr William Taylor carried to Rome was assessed by Fr Guiseppe Mazzetti O. Carm., who would later be elevated to Cardinal but was then a canon lawyer of great distinction and counsellor to Propaganda. Mazzetti's report, dated 16 July 1820, would arrive in New York only after Plessis' visit. It began with a masterful synthesis of the voluminous correspondence which had accumulated at the Vatican on the subject. It then posed two questions: first, was the current discord in New York attributable to the weakness of Bishop Connolly or the misdeeds of Charles Ffrench, and secondly, what measures needed to be taken to re-establish order in the New York church?[5] Using the same evidence that Connolly's opponents insisted illustrated Connolly's weakness, Mazzetti asserted that, far from being irresolute and feeble, Connolly accepted advice offered by proven and reliable clerics and laymen, two of whom he named as Ffrench and Cooper. As for Ffrench's alleged infamies, several questions came to mind. First, what value could be attached to witnesses in that part of the world? Did anybody know them? Was their correspondence authentic? Was their testimony notarized and worthy of being taken at face value? He pointed out that only one sworn statement, that made by Fr Louis Raby and deposed in New York without Bishop Connolly's knowledge, had been submitted in evidence and it had been based on the remarks of another person. Mazzetti commented, "Meanwhile, it is not clear who

---

[4] APF LDNA vol. 2 (1792-1830) pt. 2, 475-478, Plessis to Fontana (Quebec, 6 Sept. 1820).

[5] Voto, 4.

this charitable priest may be," then made no further reference to Raby, thereby implicitly dismissing his testimony from the case.

In fact, who was Fr Raby, who made his deposition on 6 September 1819? Raby swore that he was the pastor of Saint Antoine de Tilly, in the colony of Quebec, where he had been for five years, that he had known Ffrench for six or eight years, having met up with him when they were both in New Brunswick, and that Ffrench had lived in his house for a time. He also stated that his housekeeper had told him that in 1811 or 1812–Raby said he did not remember the exact year–while he himself was away accompanying the bishop to Quebec City, Ffrench had "wanted to seduce" her (the expression is Mazzetti's). Raby further testified that he had left Madawaska county shortly thereafter and had heard no more of Ffrench until he visited Quebec City in the summer of 1819, where he heard that Bishop Plessis had "interdicted" Ffrench in Canada in August 1817 because of immoral conduct. Raby further asserted that he had read two recent letters from Canadian clergymen on the matter and believed they told the truth; he did not name the two clergymen, nor did he say why he believed them.[6]

When one closely examines Raby's testimony, its lack of validity becomes manifest. In the first place, one is asked to believe that Raby had remained silent for several years about the affair when as a responsible and conscientious priest he was obliged to notify his bishop immediately of any such matter. Secondly, the length of time Raby says he had known Ffrench and the date of the alleged incident are not congruent, for Ffrench had stayed with Raby for only one month, in the autumn of 1812, while waiting to meet Bishop Plessis for the first time. Thirdly, the only time Ffrench could have been alone there in Raby's absence would have been after Raby and the bishop departed, yet the known facts suggest that Ffrench must have left at about the same time as the bishop's party. If not, one is

---

[6] Voto, 1-4. Plessis himself wrote that he had never interdicted Ffrench (ADC, Plessis to Angus MacEachern [Ste. Marie, 13 July 1825]).

expected to give credence to the notion that Ffrench lingered in Madawaska after the bishop and Raby had left, but that then he, a perfect stranger to the land and laden with baggage and books and obliged to retrace his steps 180 miles by canoe to Fredericton[7] before going to Quebec City himself by sea, had nevertheless arrived there almost as quickly as they, who had simply continued their voyage by river and had made no extraneous stops along the way. Raby's deposition is suspect, not only by its content but also by its singularity and by the circumstances of its creation. Although there is no doubt that Malou and Raby were in contact, the extent to which Raby's deposition was influenced by Malou can only be guessed at. However, it is significant that it is only in New York that Fr Raby put the charges on paper.[8]

Both Plessis and Maréchal came in for some sharp criticism from Mazzetti with respect to the charges against Ffrench. As we know, neither Morisset nor Plessis had investigated the initial accusation. Moreover, "there is no evidence," Mazzetti observed, "that the bishop of Quebec filed the proceedings of the case [of immorality], as he was legally required to do. And there is no

---

[7] Plessis' account of his 1812 voyage into New Brunswick refers to Fredericton as being sixty leagues from Madawaska, which is near St. Basile, with no other route between the two places than the one over which the bishop and his entourage had travelled (*Journal de deux voyages*, 275).

[8] The existence of this deposition seems to have been quickly known, for Malou made mention of it in a letter to Plessis some two months after the deposition and eight months before Mazzetti's report (AAQ EU IV no. 24 [New York, 15 Nov. 1819]). Archbishop Plessis would therefore have known about Raby's accusation long before he made his own report to Cardinal Fontana in September of the next year. Our arguments refuting Fr Raby's statements are those presented by Victor O'Daniel, in much the same terms, in his "Appendix E," 165-167. Some of O'Daniel's other arguments, however, are based on inaccurate premises or incomplete information, and his statement that "the deponent's mind was dulled and obfuscated by racial bias" is, of course, only hypothesis.

evidence that Rome was informed of these misdeeds." Only Archbishop Maréchal had forwarded some documents to Rome, sent to him by "a Quebec cleric in the service of the Quebec bishop"; these had included copies of Ffrench's exeat from the Diocese of Quebec, his discharge from his position, and Plessis' refusal to give a reason for the discharge, saying that he, Plessis, had no intention of creating one and suggesting that the friar examine his conscience.[9] "To date," Mazzetti pointed out, "it is unknown what those reasons might be."[10] When Fr Malou had

---

[9] Voto, 5-6. The "Quebec cleric in the service of the Quebec bishop" was Bishop Bernard Claude Panet, who, in his accompanying letter to Archbishop Maréchal, remarked: "By their contents you will judge what one should think of that gentleman" (AABalt case 22 G2, Panet to Maréchal [Quebec, 4 Dec. 1819]). We have not attempted to trace Panet's role in this affair, but he seems to have been more active than heretofore presumed, for in the same letter he states: "At the solicitation of several persons I had already written something about it to Monseigneur the Bishop of New York, and I believe that it was enough to engage him to revoke, or at least suspend, the powers that he gave him [Ffrench] in his Diocese. If this gentleman [Ffrench] and his partisans had protested against this severity, His Excellency would have been able to take advantage of the rumours that were circulating about him, so as to act thus with respect to him, and to require of him in addition to his *Exeat* proofs of his good conduct in Canada. For he [Ffrench] was smooth enough to obtain it before the Bishop of Quebec had received the complaints that obliged him to write him the last two letters, of which a copy is enclosed herewith."

These statements are intriguing, for they suggest that Panet had already been active in trying to oust Ffrench from his position with Connolly. His last sentence, which implies that Ffrench purposely requested his exeat so as to obtain it before a complaint could be lodged sufficient to provoke Plessis' revocation of his powers, is erroneous, for Ffrench's letter asking for an exeat is dated 14 Jan. 1816, and Morisset's report of sudden accusations of immorality was not sent until some fifteen months later.

[10] Voto, 6. To our knowledge, Plessis never did commit to paper the reasons in question, except as rare general allusions to "immorality." Even two years later he would write to Bishop MacEachern in non-

petitioned Bishop Plessis, that prelate had answered, "I know what to think of Fr Ffrench. . . ." Such a statement, Mazzetti concluded, proved nothing, and had in the event served only to restrain Malou's curiosity. Mazzetti observed further that other letters from Canada were similarly couched in general terms, one of them merely saying, "There is some truth and some falsehood in the rumours that one hears." Mazzetti then commented, "Such vague and meaningless documents are clearly insufficient to prove the accusations against Ffrench."

Mazzetti also pointed out that the Bishop of New York had received Ffrench with a valid exeat from the Bishop of Quebec, who, when Ffrench was forced to delay his departure from Canada for personal reasons, had re-appointed him to the position he had held before the exeat was granted. If Ffrench had been guilty of the crimes of which his opponents accused him, wrote Mazzetti, Bishop Plessis would not have renewed his confessional powers, adding even the power to absolve for reserved cases. Furthermore, Canadians and other priests who came to New York before Ffrench's arrival would not otherwise have praised him as they did for his zeal in building churches in several areas of Canada where the faithful were too poor to build one for themselves. Mazzetti concluded that all these facts were indications that Ffrench was *not* regarded in Canada as a bad priest, so that when he came to New York he was welcomed by all Catholics and especially by those who were now opposed to him. Indeed, if Ffrench had been guilty, Archbishop Plessis should have alerted Bishop Connolly. "So the Bishop [Connolly] was right not to prejudge him."

As for Archbishop Maréchal of Baltimore, Mazzetti's verdict was that the archbishop had done a great disservice to himself when he had sided with Malou and the trustees against Bishop Connolly, especially since he claimed not to know the whole story. Did he not himself say that church trustees

---

specific terms, saying, "I have decided for very good reasons not even to permit [Ffrench] to celebrate mass in my Diocese" (AAQ RL X no. 604 [Quebec, 2 Sept. 1822]).

everywhere in the United States displayed that same spirit of opposition to bishops? He should have known that the New York case was no different from those of Charleston, Norfolk and Philadelphia. "Did the Archbishop forget this truth, siding with the trustees against the Bishop?" Mazzetti asked. He expressed surprise at being informed that Maréchal's principle that the church should be run by the bishops rather than by the trustees should have an exception only in New York.[11] Labelling both Malou and Taylor as persons of undesirable character and noting that no one had written to the Holy See in support of Maréchal, whereas Connolly was beloved by a majority of the trustees, missionaries and congregation, Mazzetti showed clearly which side of the controversy he favoured.

In short, Mazzetti supported Connolly and Cooper in the quarrel at St. Peter's, chastized Taylor and Malou soundly, admonished Archbishops Plessis and Maréchal, and reproached others who had acted peripherally in the affair. As for Charles Dominic Ffrench, although Mazzetti seemed fully to approve of his activities in the quarrel with the trustees, his judgment remained prudent: "On the other hand, since Father Ffrench has not been cleared of his accusations, and of his reputation of being a bad priest, the Bishop should be told to allow him discreetly to depart from the city of New York, but not before the matter is settled."[12]

The troubles in New York continued for another year. After a further review of the case, Rome finally rendered its decision. Propaganda instructed Connolly to order Malou to leave the Diocese of New York *quam primum*, under penalty of suspension *a divinis* and the loss of all his missionary faculties, but he refused. Eventually suspended from the Diocese of New York, Malou was ordered by his Provincial to return to his Jesuit community but refused to obey that order, too, choosing to stay

---

[11] Voto, 5-7.
[12] Voto, 8.

on in New York instead. He was then expelled from his Order, but was subsequently reinstated. Fr William Taylor, who had presented the interests of the old wardens to Rome, was suspended from all sacerdotal powers as soon as he reappeared in New York, and the Sacred Congregation confirmed Bishop Connolly's sentence on him; he was ultimately rescued from this ignominy by Bishop Jean-Louis de Cheverus of Boston. As for Ffrench, the judgment against him was much more lenient. Propaganda ordered Connolly to counsel Ffrench discreetly to leave the diocese, for the sake of peace, within three months following receipt of the directive; this action was to be taken only if Malou and Taylor were ordered away. Should Ffrench refuse to leave he would be suspended, unless his departure would create a scandal.[13]

Mazzetti seems clearly to have had grave reservations with respect to Ffrench's guilt. Certainly, he appears to have doubted the veracity of the charges against him, but Ffrench had either been unable or unwilling to prove his innocence, so that his reputation as an unworthy priest had not been fully rehabilitated. In other words, Ffrench may have been innocent, but no proof of his innocence had been submitted. Indeed, the modern concept of "innocent until proven guilty" seems to have played no role whatsoever in Ffrench's life, at this or any earlier stage of his career.

Ffrench availed himself of his privilege to continue on in New York for the whole three months, and Bishop Connolly welcomed the continuation of his services for even this short period. Ffrench also used the time to prepare his return to Saint John. By then he had determined that all the allegations against him had originated in New Brunswick, and his purpose in going there was to ascertain the precise nature and the sources of the charges. What no doubt also encouraged him in his decision to make the journey was that, almost a year earlier, the Saint John

---

[13] APF L e D vol. 302 fol. 252rv, Propaganda to Connolly (Rome, 18 Aug. 1821); Ryan, *Old St. Peter's*, 150-154; Dignan, "Peter Anthony Malou," 84.

congregation had written to him asking that he return to them. Not knowing that Fr Morisset had now been appointed to the mission, Ffrench thus saw in its invitation a possible opportunity to earn his bread while he was there. It will be recalled that after the departure of Fr McQuade in the summer of 1818 the congregation had remained untended. On 26 May 1821 Philip Kehoe had pleaded with Plessis for a resident pastor, asserting that his own letter to the prelate was merely the most recent one on the subject.[14] In order to have financial support during his quest, Ffrench therefore appealed once more to Archbishop Plessis for faculties in the Diocese of Quebec.

His letter is dated 18 January 1822. Its first statement touched on the accusation that he was "an enemy of the French nation" or had spoken "in a very disrespectful manner of the Venerable French Prelates and Priests of the United States." To this charge he stated emphatically that all assertions of the kind were false and unfounded and that no man would say so to his face. He also referred to allegations that he was the cause of all the troubles that had lately distracted the congregation of New York. Instead, he insisted, it was the trustees who were to blame, by claiming the right to rule not only the temporals but also the spirituals of the church. Ffrench commented:

> Had your Grace a true knowledge of the more than disgraceful transactions of New-York, and the injuries offered to Religion by the *unchristian*, the *unjust* and *malevolent* Conduct of an insignif[ic]ant and rebellious few . . . the conduct I have pursued throughout the whole of this most trying conflict, would have met with, instead of censure, your most decided approbation. This assertion may appear rather strong, but there can be no difference of opinion, between your Grace and me on this head, it is no more no less, than the authority of the Church and the support of its discipline.

---

[14] AAQ NB II no. 27, Kehoe to Plessis (Saint John, 26 May 1821).

Finally he assured the bishop that he had been "more than four years in this City, and no Clergyman stands higher in public estimation nor higher in the good opinion of all Classes and Denomination of Christians." Given these circumstances, he was requesting that he be granted faculties in New Brunswick. Accompanying this letter was one from Bishop Connolly commending Ffrench for faculties in the Quebec diocese.[15]

Plessis had long since ceased to answer Ffrench's letters, but on 23 February 1822 he did write to Bishop Connolly, saying that Ffrench would not get faculties or even permission to say mass in his diocese. He asked Connolly to dissuade Ffrench from his proposed undertaking, especially since "a good and virtuous Canadian priest" (Fr Joseph Morisset) was now pastor at Saint John and he, Plessis, preferred him to "a vagabond monk from whom there is little good and much evil to expect."[16] Unfortunately, Archbishop Plessis did not ask Connolly actually to notify the Dominican of the contents of his letter, and it seems that Connolly did not do so, not even of the fact that Plessis had refused Ffrench permission to offer mass. Ffrench's ignorance of Plessis' sweeping refusal was to cause much turmoil when he did return to Saint John. The depth of Plessis' decided antagonism towards Ffrench is expressed in the prelate's own hand in a scrawl along the top of Ffrench's letter to him: "He exculpates himself, the true cause of the schism among the Catholics."[17] These words can mean only that Plessis still deemed Ffrench to be the cause of the disorder in New York, even though the troubles had begun before Ffrench's arrival and though Ffrench himself had taken the position there of asserting the authority of

---

[15] AAQ EU IV no. 35, Ffrench to Plessis (New York, 18 Jan. 1822). Plessis would assume that Ffrench's principal motive in coming to New Brunswick was to take charge of a mission, but all the written documents indicate that any such motive was secondary to Ffrench's desire to re-establish his reputation.
[16] AAQ RL X no. 506, Plessis to Connolly (Quebec, 23 Feb. 1822).
[17] AAQ EU IV no. 35, Ffrench to Plessis (New York, 18 Jan. 1822).

the bishop in all spiritual matters. It is indeed a curious fact that Archbishop Plessis, who was himself a strong proponent of ecclesiastical authority, should hold Fr Ffrench so much in abhorrence that he would prefer to side, in this issue, with those who sought to diminish that authority as much as possible.

On the other hand, Bishop Henry Conwell of Philadelphia heard of Ffrench's intention to leave New York and offered him a post in his diocese. Ffrench thanked him for the offer but decided to postpone any acceptance until he had completed his visit to New Brunswick.[18] The Board of Trustees of St. Peter's then formalized this testimonial to its departing pastor:

> Resolved that we cannot Suffer the Rev. Charles Ffrench to retire from the Situation he holds as Pastor of this Church without an Acknowledgment of his Exemplary Conduct and usefulness in his Ministry, during a term of Five Years, and an Expression of our unfeigned Regret in his Removal and the Hope which we fondly Cherish that the Separation will not be of Long Duration.[19]

For some reason, Archbishop Plessis seems to have been under a misunderstanding at this time with respect to Propaganda's decision to restore peace in New York by sending both Ffrench and Malou away, for in a letter to Bishop Jean Jacques Lartigue in November of 1821 he wrote, "You recall perhaps that I had written to Dr Conelly that the only way to re-establish peace in his church was to send away Messrs French and Malou. He did not follow this advice with respect to the former, contenting himself with depriving the other of his powers."[20] Is it possible that Plessis had simply not yet heard that Ffrench was to leave

---

[18] *American Catholic Historical Researches* 8: 1 (Jan. 1891), 67, Ffrench to Conwell (New York, 7 Feb. 1822).
[19] Ryan, *Old St. Peter's*, 154, quoting *Minute Book of St. Peter's*, April 3, 1820 to April 1, 1823.
[20] AAQ RL X no. 469, Plessis to Lartigue (Quebec, 26 Nov. 1821).

New York in a few months, too? Even if this were the case, so that the Quebec prelate felt that Ffrench had been treated too leniently in comparison with Malou, his obduracy with respect to Ffrench at this time is difficult to understand in view of the lack of evidence against him and the support Ffrench continued to receive in so many other quarters, including Rome. Equally mysterious is his preference for the disgraced Malou, to whom he would offer a post, albeit a minor one, in his diocese less than two months later. Malou would decline the offer, citing reasons of health.[21]

Despite the Quebec prelate's generous gesture, Malou would eventually turn against Plessis as well. Some three years after Plessis' offer of a position, he would write to the Prefect of Propaganda as follows: "It is to the report of Monseigneur of Quebec that I owe my sad and painful situation. . . . Monseigneur of Quebec feared that matters would be brought before the tribunals, where we would have been obliged to produce his own letters and those of several of his priests, which outlined the infamy of French's conduct in the diocese of Quebec. He persuaded himself wrongly that by ousting both of us he would get rid of this uneasiness, for if at that moment I had left, the sane part of the congregation, already too fired up, would have gone to extremes, which I have always prevented by my influence and my advice in favour of moderation." Malou's claim to be a proponent of moderation would have astonished even Archbishop Plessis, who, in his report to Cardinal Fontana, had remarked that the Jesuit was "fanning the flames" during the trustee controversy in New York.[22]

---

[21] AAQ RL X no. 487, Plessis to Malou (Quebec, 7 Jan. 1822); AAQ EU IV no. 36, Malou to Plessis (New York, 20 Jan. 1822). See also AAQ RL X no. 488, Plessis to John Power (Quebec, 7 Jan. 1822).

[22] APF SOCG-SP vols. 935-948 (1825-1833), fols. 114r-115v, Malou to Prefect of Propaganda (New York, 14 Feb. 1825); APF LDNA vol. 2 (1792-1830) pt. 2, 475-478, Plessis to Fontana (Quebec, 6 Sept. 1820).

View of the City of Saint John, 1827, by A. Robinson after Henry Hunt. Courtesy New Brunswick Museum, Saint John, N.B. (W6760).

Chapter 6

DISCOVERIES AND DISAPPOINTMENTS: NEW BRUNSWICK (1822-1826)

On 12 April 1822, Ffrench took passage for Saint John on the British ship *Spectator*. Two days out, off Montauk Point, Long Island, the craft sprang a leak and quickly filled up with water. Passengers and crew–twenty-seven souls in all–took to the longboats about fifteen miles south of Newport Light, making it ashore near Newport, Rhode Island, after twelve hours on heavy seas in a thick fog. Ffrench lost all of his library, much of his baggage, and almost all of his papers and valuables. He then made his way to Boston by road, where he was warmly welcomed and succoured by Bishop Cheverus and the clerical members of his household. Among the latter was Fr William Taylor, one of Ffrench's principal foes during the trustee wars in New York and now Vicar General of the Boston Diocese. Given their previous relationship, one would expect a pronounced coolness to exist between the two men, but such was not the case. Instead, Ffrench wrote soon afterwards that his former enemy not only treated him "with great civility" but that he and Taylor "have forgotten all past controversies and are become mutual and cordial friends." Ffrench also gratefully thanked a number of laymen, five of whom he named and who quite probably arranged for the replacement of his lost clothing and personal effects. It appears that Ffrench remained in Boston for several days. When a suitable craft became available for passage to Saint John he was joined by the bishop and his clergy as they extended their best wishes and farewells.[1]

---

[1] *City Gazette* [Saint John], 1 May 1822; "Conversion," 32-37; Georgetown University Archives, *A Short Memoir, with some*

In a published document, Ffrench described how he was greeted upon arrival in Saint John by a large delegation of the City's citizens, including members of every religious denomination. He took advantage of the occasion to commend the non-Catholics of the City, saying they were a "kind, unprejudiced and hospitable people refined in their manners; they have been very partial to me and have contributed very liberally towards the building of our church." He then outlined the sequence of events that had occurred in the New York congregation over the previous four years, and itemized the accusations levelled against him. Much chagrined by what they had heard, the Saint John Catholics proposed several methods of redress but, upon Ffrench being called to Norton on urgent business regarding his property there,[2] the members of the Congregation met without him several times. Then, on his return to the City, they presented him with an affidavit signed by 126

Documents in Vindication of the Charges made by Malicious Persons Against the Character of the Rev. Charles Ffrench, addressed to the Roman Catholics of British America, and of the United States, 5 Aug. 1822, 5-6. The entire text of the latter document, herein referred to as *A Short Memoir*, can be found in Appendix A of this study. Pagination indicated in references to it is that of the original, not of the transcribed text.

This was not Ffrench's only first-hand experience of the perils of ocean travel. During his return voyage from Portugal to Ireland in 1801, the ship he was on narrowly escaped being capsized by a storm, only to be captured the next day by privateers. Ffrench and his fellow passengers were then put off, unharmed, on the Spanish coast, from where they made their way back to Portugal, eventually to take passage on another ship. Ffrench's account of the incident can be found in his "Conversion," 21-24.

[2] *A Short Memoir*, 6. Ffrench's farm had been seized by the sheriff and was about to be sold for the benefit of persons who had sworn, in his absence, that he owed them money. Ffrench was in time to prevent the sale, and the court found in his favour, ruling that, instead of owing money, Ffrench was actually owed five shillings ten pence.

communicants, the purpose of which was to recognize formally his edifying conduct during his time in Saint John.

The document further stated that only recently had the source of the most grievous slander of Ffrench's character been discovered, namely one Richard Toole, "on whose testimony the smallest reliance cannot be placed, being a man of foul character, and prone to intemperance and unblushing immorality." Such is, the affidavit proclaimed, "the man who had the audacity to address the most Rev. Bishops of Quebec and New-York, on a subject of infamy and falsehood!!!" Appended to this deposition were two letters written by Mary Toole, Richard Toole's spouse. The first was an apology to Ffrench for having falsely denounced him to Bishops Plessis and Connolly, while the second was effectively a certificate outlining the reasons that had led her to libel Ffrench; it was duly witnessed by two reputable members of the Congregation. Mrs Toole stated that, under threat of death from her husband, who had been the recipient of bribes from a man in New York, she had in the past been forced to write a letter asserting scandalous falsehoods about Ffrench.[3]

Mrs Toole now also wrote to both Archbishop Plessis and Bishop Connolly, beginning her letter in the following terms:

> I am the unhappy woman who wrote several letters to your Lordship setting forth scandalous calumnies of the Revd. Mr Ffrench. I know in this I have committed a great fault but what I hope will in some degree lessen it in your eyes is that I was forced to write what was worded to me by my husband Richard Toole, he had a knife drawn and threatened to plunge it into my breast dare I to refuse to comply, he planned the story so naturally and with such a deal of artifice that it bore the appearance of truth, he also planned a letter as if writting in New York by Mr Ffrench addressed to me in which he Mr Ffrench seemed to acknowledge bad conduct with a woman in Miramichi, and praying me to send her to him with

---

[3] *A Short Memoir*, 7-11.

her Child in the New York Packet, it is to be regretted the letter so Planned was destroyed, as the forgery could be proved . . . it was said some Person from New York who was an enemy to Mr Ffrench Bribed him to injure Mr Ffrench's Character who was loved and revered by all who knew him in this Quarter and who always distinguished himself for his zeal in the Cause of Religion. . . .[4]

Her long letter is dated 6 June 1822. At the time it was written, the woman's husband had left the area and the identity of the person who bribed him could, and presumably still can, only be guessed at.

No archival material has been found to indicate that Plessis ever replied to Mrs Toole's letter, nor has any trace been found of the several other letters she alluded to above. However, while writing to Fr Morisset, Plessis mentioned having received this letter from Mrs Toole and stated that he had already had two previous letters from her.[5]

In *A Short Memoir*, Ffrench also referred to a sworn statement that he had obtained in New York; this document asserted that, insofar as the woman who claimed that he had fathered her child was concerned, Ffrench did not and could not have been in her presence at any time for the conception to have taken place. The statement had been signed by one James Stack before Judge Swanton of the Marine Court and Notary in New York. Stack, whom Ffrench had known in the Miramichi, was well thought of by both Fr Morisset at Saint John and Fr Phillip Lariscy O.S.A. of Boston. According to Ffrench, Connolly had received a copy of this document but his own original had been lost in the shipwreck off the coast of Maine.[6]

---

[4] AAQ NB II no. 36, Mary Toole to Plessis (Saint John, 6 June 1822).
[5] AAQ RL X no. 607 (Quebec, 4 Sept. 1822).
[6] *A Short Memoir*, 12-13. We have been unable to locate Connolly's copy of this document, if it still exists.

Ch. 6. Discoveries and Disappointments 97

It is clear that Ffrench had begun obtaining proofs of his innocence even before leaving New York. Now, having strong evidence of a conspiracy against him, linking events in New York with those at Saint John and events at Saint John with those in the Miramichi, he proceeded to the latter settlement in search of the woman involved. He went first to Bay du Vin but finally found her at Miramichi, where she was now living with her non-Catholic husband. Ffrench wrote that her former neighbours at Bay du Vin had spoken of her as being "of bad character, that she had several children by different persons (who are now known) before she was married, and they are of opinion that she must be either influenced by some enemy to speak of me as she did, or she had engaged in it, as a design or scheme to get money." Ffrench confronted her personally, and attempted to persuade her to repudiate her charge before a magistrate, but to no avail.[7]

On the other hand, everywhere he turned now, in New Brunswick, Ffrench seemed to find people willing to act as witnesses to his good character. John English, a patriarch of the Miramichi and a great benefactor of the church, gathered 49 signatures to a testimonial which extolled Ffrench's "uniform conduct [and] his unostentatious piety." This despite the fact that Mr English and Fr Ffrench had not been on good terms for many months during the latter's early ministry. The document also stated, "The report, which the tongue of slander endeavoured to obtain belief for, was only believed by a few, we never gave any credit to it, and now there is scarcely any person who would ever speak of it, since certain circumstances have come to light, but as a matter of imposition and fraud." The French-speaking communities of Bay du Vin and Neguac added their own praise and memorial, the latter's being presented by Otho Robichaud, a highly regarded justice of the peace. It insisted, "As for the tongue of slander it did not prevail with us, we never believed

---

[7] *A Short Memoir*, 13-14; AAQ NB VI no. 76, Cooke to Plessis (Bartibog, 5 Aug. 1822).

the malicious and lying report. May God forgive the authors of it. The Rev. Charles Ffrench's conduct while amongst us was truly pious, regular and exemplary." Of the 28 signatures to this memorial, four bear the same surname as the woman who had defied Ffrench, and all were from Bay du Vin, and so almost certainly her relatives of one degree or another."[8]

Unfortunately, Ffrench could not claim that support for him was universal. Among those who seem not to have been completely persuaded of his innocence was Fr Thomas Cooke, the missionary at Nipisiguit and later the first bishop of Trois Rivières. Relating Ffrench's failure to persuade the woman at Bay du Vin to recant, Cooke wrote to Plessis, "A great portion of the community does not believe her and I approve of them a lot, whatever my private ideas may be." Then, although he was not himself familiar with the mission at Saint John, he added, "He [Ffrench] has too many enemies ever to remain there as missionary."[9]

Ffrench returned to Saint John shortly after he had gathered together his testimonials and visited friends along the Miramichi. On 5 August 1822 he appended a short apologia to the document and delivered the whole to Henry Chubb at the *City Gazette* office for printing. The result was the sixteen-page pamphlet bearing the title *A Short Memoir, with some Documents in Vindication of the Charges made by Malicious Persons Against the Character of the Rev. Charles Ffrench, addressed to the Roman Catholics of British America and of the United States*. On 11 September he addressed another letter to Archbishop Plessis, in which he gently chided the prelate for not having written to him, pointing out that it was only on his return to New Brunswick that he himself had become fully informed of the real nature of the charges against his character. At the same time he

---

[8] *A Short Memoir*, 14-15. For details about Ffrench's strained relations with John English, see AAQ NB VI no. 143, Ffrench to Plessis (30 May 1815); AAQ NB VI no. 144, Ffrench to Plessis (20 Oct. 1815); AAQ NB VI no. 145, Ffrench to Plessis (14 Jan. 1816).

[9] AAQ NB VI no. 76, Cooke to Plessis (Bartibog, 5 Aug. 1822).

conceded that Plessis' attitude was understandable, since any priest "who would have abused to such a degree the confidence placed in him . . . should not expect any mark of attention from him." Then he added, "However, if *all these charges* were false as I most solemnly declare they are, can your Lordship think it ill that I again take the liberty of writing to you. I could scarcely believe it. I flatter myself that you will not consider it too much presumption in me, to present your Lordship with the little pamphlet I have just published in vindication of my Character."[10]

Plessis neither responded to the note nor acknowledged that he had received the *Memoir*, save to Fr Cooke, to whom he forwarded the document. After that, no trace of the *Memoir* itself was found in the diocesan archives until after the writers of this study had placed a copy there. Plessis was still unwilling to investigate the matter or to accept that there could exist any genuine evidence that Ffrench was other than guilty. In fact, he seems to have assumed that the document was fraudulent. As he wrote to Cooke, "To hear him [Ffrench], he is as innocent as when he was baptised. . . . I have difficulty in believing that he obtained at Nigaouek and Bartabog all the signatures that his pamphlet carries."[11] Plessis' own earlier dictum that no one should be condemned until proven guilty seems to have completely slipped his mind. Indeed, he appears to have alerted the clergy in and near the Saint John and Miramichi missions

---

[10] AAQ NB II no. 39, Ffrench to Plessis (Saint John, 11 Sept. 1822).

[11] AAQ RL XI no. 32, Plessis to Cooke (Quebec, 13 Oct. 1822). In his reply to Plessis, Fr Cooke wrote that the memoir was "not a thing to show around," and he expressed the opinion that it had not been made public (AAQ NB VI no. 82 [Neguac and Miramichi, 24 Feb. 1823]). The fact that Plessis doubted the authenticity of the document is astonishing, given the unlikelihood that anyone who published such controversial material would expect to have it taken seriously unless it were based on a widely recognized reality, especially when it used the services of a well-known public printer and contained so many signatures susceptible of verification or denial.

that Ffrench was in their neighbourhood, and warned them against him.[12]

At the time that instruction was issued, Fr Joseph Morisset had been pastor in Saint John since the middle of 1821. He had more than once told Plessis that he was very unhappy there and wanted to get away from the Irish, clergy as well as laity.[13] In early October 1822, he wrote the archbishop that Ffrench had been in Saint John since May and that he had seen nothing reprehensible in his conduct since his arrival. In fact, Morisset suggested to Plessis that he engage Ffrench to sell his properties at Saint John and go to Canada (Quebec). "Your Excellency," he suggested, "could make an excellent subject of Mr Ffrench by treating him gently and by showing confidence in him." A month later, "the people like [Ffrench] but do not appear to want him as their pastor." Plessis, of course, did not encourage Morisset in such ideas, and Morisset seems to have trodden a delicate diplomatic line in this respect, for he confessed to Plessis that he never walked with Ffrench in public but that he welcomed him pleasantly whenever he came to his house. "The advice you give me," he wrote to Plessis, "will make me accord him a colder reception," and "I have always been distrustful of him, and I do not think I have compromised myself."[14] But in reply to any and all of Morisset's suggestions that Ffrench be treated more leniently Plessis remained deaf, writing in reply, "This man has left a bad smell everywhere he has been. . . . If this religious is kept in New Brunswick only by the hope of being employed

---

[12] AAQ RL X no. 604, Plessis to MacEachern (Quebec, 2 Sept. 1822); AAQ RL X no. 607, Plessis to Morisset (Quebec, 4 Sept. 1822); AAQ RL XI no. 32, Plessis to Cooke (Quebec, 13 Oct. 1822).

[13] For instance, see AAQ NB II no. 28, Morisset to Plessis (Saint John, 23 July 1821); AAQ NB II no. 30, Morisset to Plessis (Saint John, Sept. 1821); AAQ NB II no. 35, Morisset to Plessis (Saint John, 2 April 1822); AAQ NB II no. 40, Morisset to Plessis (Saint John, 6 Oct. 1822).

[14] AAQ NB II no. 40, Morisset to Plessis (Saint John, 6 Oct. 1822); AAQ NB II no. 41, Morisset to Plessis (Saint John, 6 Nov. 1822).

there one day, he can pack his bags right now. The diocese has no need of his services."[15]

It will be recalled that, immediately on receiving the first allegation of Ffrench's fall from grace, Plessis had revoked his authority to preach and administer the sacraments. The faculties referred to here were those extended on 5 November 1816 and included authority in certain reserved cases. There was no mention yet, however, of any suspension or withdrawal of Ffrench's right to say mass. When McQuade had looked over the document he had told Ffrench that the prohibition encompassed that right, but Ffrench was unsure. Still, Ffrench had bent over backwards to comply, promising Plessis, "I will refrain until I hear from your Lordship tho such a prohibition dont appear to me to be contained in yr letter." In fact, in Plessis' final letter to the Dominican, dated 26 August 1817, he explicitly stated that Ffrench was not forbidden to say mass, but was advised to refrain from doing so until after a long penance.[16] These were among the documents that Archbishop Maréchal had forwarded to Rome later on, Plessis being absent in Europe at the time. When replying to Bishop Connolly's recommendation that he grant faculties to Fr Ffrench upon his return to New Brunswick in 1822, Plessis had not only refused to grant them but had said that he would not even give Ffrench permission to say mass.[17]

In the summer of 1824, Fr Michael Carroll replaced Fr Morisset as missionary at Saint John. At about this time, too, Fr Ffrench became concerned about his finances. With few means of support apart from the "living" that Carroll is reputed to have given him,[18] he decided to open a school for the education of Catholic youth. In view of his excellent rapport with the Protestant community, it is not surprising that he welcomed the

---

[15] AAQ RL XI no. 105, Plessis to Morisset (Quebec, 27 Dec. 1822).

[16] AAQ NB II no. 13, Ffrench to Plessis (Saint John, 21 July 1817); AAQ RL IX no. 201, Plessis to Ffrench (Quebec, 26 Aug. 1817).

[17] AAQ RL X no. 506, Plessis to Connolly (Quebec, 23 Feb. 1822).

[18] AAQ NB III no. 105, Louis Gingras to Plessis (Memramcook, 23 Feb. 1825).

children of non-Catholics into his academy as well. Little is known about this institution.[19] The following December, Ffrench informed Plessis that his Academy was assuming an air of great notice and respectability, that it afforded him a decent living, and that the inhabitants of all persuasions were most anxious to erect a small chapel "at their own expense and bounty." He suggested to Plessis that he could be of some service in looking to the instruction of the children and the poor servants who could not attend the parochial mass, for St. Malachy's was now too small, "not capable of containing very little more than half the Congregation." He made no mention of the fact that, scarcely ten years before, Plessis had been annoyed that the new church promised to be too large![20]

That Ffrench had agreed to the offer of the chapel and apparently had Carroll's support in the matter, might at first seem surprising under the circumstances, but the straightforward way in which he makes his case suggests that he was completely confident of his own integrity in the matter of the allegations levelled against him. It also supports the evidence that Bishop Connolly had not communicated to him all of Plessis' response on his request for faculties, and specifically the prelate's refusal to permit him to say mass if he returned to New Brunswick, even temporarily, in an effort to exonerate himself. Clearly, Ffrench's belief that he was free to perform the liturgy was based on the contents of Plessis' last letter to him more than seven years

---

[19] The school with its attached chapel was called The Friary. When the building ceased being used for educational and religious purposes, it continued to serve other functions in Saint John until its destruction in the great fire of 1877. One of the earliest public notices of The Friary dates from 28 May 1825, when the *New-Brunswick Courier* reported that the frame of a chapel was being raised on one of Fr Ffrench's lots on Horsfield Street, and that work on the structure was drawing "many persons of every persuasion in this city." In a written document (see Appendix D), Ffrench stated that his school had 70 Protestant students in addition to its Catholic students.

[20] AAQ NB II no. 59, Ffrench to Plessis (Saint John, 2 Dec. 1824).

previously, for he had received no official directive from Plessis since that time; so far as he knew, therefore, that remnant of his faculties was still in force. Indeed, Fr Michael Carroll, on the strength of Plessis' letter of 26 August 1817, which revoked Ffrench's faculties but expressly allowed him to say mass, had already extended him that privilege in Saint John.[21]

Fr Carroll's unexpected death on 24 November 1824, after only a few months at Saint John, placed a very Catholic and public burden on Ffrench's shoulders, a burden which he accepted with no little care and reverence. While it is true that Plessis' prohibitions on Ffrench's priestly functions were extensive, they were limited, in any event, by the canonical exception expressed in the phrase *in articulo mortis*. Consequently, Ffrench attended Carroll's deathbed, bestowed the last rites, offered the funeral mass, and undertook extensive preparations for his burial. The funeral was held from St. Malachy's and was the largest attended in the City up to that time. A large number of people walked in the procession to the Burying Ground in Portland Parish. As the attendant clergyman, Fr Ffrench preceded the pallbearers, who were the six clergymen of the several Protestant congregations, wearing their ecclesiastical garb. Then followed the mourners of the parish, the attending physicians, the military commanders, and elements of the Saint John garrison. Via the local newspapers, Fr Ffrench formally thanked those in attendance, and commended as "gentlemen of liberality and goodness" those who took part.[22]

His report to Plessis of Carroll's demise was dated 2 December 1824. In it Ffrench gave a short description of the latter's edifying death, as well as of the sorrow and repentance of those in attendance. His message ended with a plea for more equitable treatment at the bishop's hands: "[I] would appeal to the purity of yr own heart, whether (after the justification I have

---

[21] AAQ NB II no. 69, Church Wardens of St. Malachy's to Plessis (Saint John, 17 March 1825).
[22] SCAR, Charles Ffrench dossier, doc. 2 (*City Gazette* [Saint John], 2 Dec. 1824).

so satisfactorily given of my Character) have I been well treated or not." He noted that the congregation had requested him to take charge of the chapel but that he had declined, being quite satisfied with his present project of the academy. He promised, however, that he would do for them what he could until a pastor —and he suggested it be an *Irish* pastor—was appointed.[23]

At a general meeting of the parishioners of St. Malachy's, a resolution was adopted that a committee of seven be appointed to manage the temporalities of the congregation for one year. A second proposal returned thanks to Fr Ffrench for his services to the late pastor, while a third resolution delegated the chairman of the meeting to meet with Fr Ffrench and invite him to accept their unanimous call to be their pastor. Finally, a committee of three was appointed to compose a memorial to Archbishop Plessis, soliciting him to sanction their choice. In it, they stated, "[Knowing that] your Lordship was unfavourable to him [Ffrench], in consequence of some impressions made on your mind, by some evil minded persons, which excited in them a desire to watch his conduct more minutely than they would otherwise have done, and . . . after a long residence amongst them, under such scrutinizing observations, they are happy to say, that his character as a Minister of the Gospel, stands higher than ever (if possible) in their estimation."[24]

The measure of the favour in which Ffrench was held by the Congregation at St. Malachy's is best illustrated by the number of communications requesting his appointment as pastor. No less than four were prepared and forwarded to Quebec in the half year immediately following Fr Carroll's death.[25] These were

---

[23] AAQ NB II no. 59, Ffrench to Plessis (Saint John, 2 Dec. 1824).

[24] AAQ NB II no. 60, Saint John Catholics to Plessis (Saint John, 15 Dec. 1824); SCAR, Charles Ffrench dossier, doc. 3 (*New-Brunswick Courier*, 11 Dec. 1824, "Catholic Meeting").

[25] The four memorials are dated 15 Dec. 1824, 12 Jan. 1825, 29 Jan. 1825, and 17 March 1825. According to Fr Louis Gingras, some members of the Saint John congregation believed that any complaints

Ch. 6. Discoveries and Disappointments   105

invariably expressed in cordial and dutiful terms, although in one or two instances a note of frustration peeks through. It seems that at least one of them caused some offence as well, when it asserted, "[The congregation expresses its] sorrow in hearing that you support a correspondence with a Grogg Seller and Mr. M's washerwomen in this City; as there are several respectable characters among us here with whom you might correspond without being liable to the petulant remarks of several who are not your friends." Even if this reproach had not been based on a misunderstanding–it had been a Mr Griffiths rather than Fr Morisset's washerwoman, a Mrs Griffiths, who had been in contact with the archbishop–it was not a tactic destined to further the wardens' cause.[26] The fourth successive memorial pointed out that the need for a pastor was so great that some Catholics were attending Protestant services and even being married by a Protestant minister, that, in fact, Plessis' permission for Ffrench to serve for only a temporary three-month period would be welcome.[27] But Plessis did not bend. For his part, Ffrench did not once accept the wardens' offer, although he appears to have offered his services for mass.

New reports thus reached Plessis that Ffrench had been offering mass at St. Malachy's ever since the death of Fr Carroll.[28] By early 1825, Plessis was referring to Ffrench as an intruder-priest, and stating that he was in danger of exposing himself to a charge of irregularity if he continued to preach and say mass. He also asked Fr William Dollard, then missionary on

---

made against Fr Morisset were the product of Ffrench's intrigues (AAQ NB III no. 105, Gingras to Plessis [Memramcook, 23 Feb. 1825]).

[26] AAQ NB II no. 63, Church Wardens of St. Malachy's to Plessis (Saint John, 12 Jan. 1825). The error about the washerwoman was quickly corrected in a letter to the wardens from Plessis' secretary (AAQ RL XII no. 183, N.C. Fortier to Toole et al. [Quebec, 3 March 1825]).

[27] AAQ NB II no. 69, Trustees of St. Malachy's to Plessis (Saint John, 17 March 1825).

[28] As in AAQ NB VI no. 162, Dollard to Plessis (5 Feb. 1825).

the Miramichi and later Bishop of New Brunswick, to visit Saint John, in order to assess the situation and to report back.[29] In the meantime a letter from Plessis to the Saint John congregation apparently persuaded Ffrench to stop saying mass.[30] According to Peter McNamara, likely the chief churchwarden at the time, the trustees then took possession of the chapel, locked its doors, and intended to keep the keys until the archbishop sent a pastor.[31]

Dollard wrote to Plessis from Saint John on 9 June 1825, informing him that Ffrench was no longer saying mass in St. Malachy's but was holding the keys to the vestments and tabernacle until such time as a pastor arrived. Dollard asked one of the committee to go and demand the keys, but Ffrench gave them over without being asked. Much of what Dollard told Plessis seems to have been exaggerated. It is clear that he went to Saint John with a negative mind-set towards Ffrench. He also seems to have been fearful of him, for Ffrench tried to see Dollard on at least two occasions but was put off, on the first occasion by Dollard's excuse that he was preparing for mass, and on the second by the latter's taking refuge in his breviary immediately after the mass. It was only because of a chance meeting that they spent some time in speaking and apparently there was at least one heated exchange of views. Two weeks later, Dollard again wrote to Plessis, "[Ffrench] thinks he can safely say mass," and "[he] threatened to sue me for defamation of character, as I had, according to your Lordship's instructions, made known the contrary to the people."[32]

---

[29] AAQ RL XII no. 153, Plessis to MacEachern (Quebec, 13 Jan. 1825); AAQ RL XII no. 160, Plessis to Dollard (Quebec, 27 Jan. 1825); AAQ RL XII no. 231, Plessis to Lartigue (Quebec, 26 April 1825).

[30] AAQ NB II no. 60a, Plessis to the Church Wardens of St. Malachy's (Quebec, 12 Jan. 1825).

[31] AAQ NB II no. 73, Peter McNamara et al. to Plessis (Saint John, 5 May 1825).

[32] AAQ NB II no. 74, Dollard to Plessis (Saint John, 9 June 1825); AAQ NB II no. 75, Dollard to Plessis (Fredericton, 22 June 1825).

Dollard's statements are worth examining. Argument has already been offered that Ffrench was surely convinced of his own innocence, that he was not suspended, and that the last letter he had received from the bishop permitted him to say mass.[33] All of these factors supported his conviction that he could "safely" offer mass. Given these conditions, to suggest that he would actually threaten such a suit as Dollard mentions beggars the imagination. First of all, there was no reason for him to do so, since most of the congregation had now heard that he had no permission to offer mass. Secondly, though it would not be the first lawsuit Ffrench had initiated, he knew that canon law strictly forbade any cleric from being dragged into court, and there can be no doubt that he was fully aware that, should he embark on such a course in the Diocese of Quebec, he would surely be suspended or even defrocked.[34] Considering all these factors, Dollard's reports demand rejection as statements of fact, especially as he may easily have misinterpreted Ffrench's words, which, under the circumstances, might very well have become quite heated. He further recorded that Ffrench was in the middle of building a chapel "of considerable dimensions, 58 feet by 40, to which I am informed the late Mr Carroll became the first subscriber." Dollard added, "I am sorry to say that, the rest of his conduct here was nothing inferior to this, either in imprudence or folly, so that, on the whole, it has produced here evils that, I fear, will not be very speedily remidied. . . . All reasoning is lost on a

---

[33] One of the trustees' memorials to Plessis had stated quite cogently Ffrench's reasons for assuming he could say mass: "Mr Ffrench has all along declared that your last letter to him in 1817, allowed him to say the *Holy Mass*; and the Revd Mr. Carroll also sanctioned him in the performance of that office" (AAQ NB II no. 69 [Saint John, 17 March 1825]). A half-dozen lines to Ffrench from Plessis himself might quickly have settled this particular matter at any time during the four-year period between 1822 and 1826, but this simple act the archbishop seemed loath to perform.

[34] The authors owe these particular arguments to Victor O'Daniel. See his "Appendix E," 188-189.

man of this kind; and it is to be feared that except some means be adopted, that he and his chapel will still create discord and dissentions. . . ."[35] Dollard did not say why he thought Ffrench's chapel would create discord and dissension and, indeed, no such results were recorded.

It is significant that, despite his apprehensions and his predisposition against the Dominican from the beginning, Dollard never mentions in any of his correspondence the alleged Bay du Vin affair. Since he had been stationed in the Miramichi for nine years and so must have known the people there, Dollard therefore almost certainly placed no credence in the charges emanating from that quarter. He remained in Saint John until Fr Patrick McMahon, the new pastor, arrived in the City on 16 June 1825.[36]

That McMahon arrived in Saint John with the same preconceived view of Fr Ffrench as had Fr Dollard can be seen in his first letter to Plessis, dated 14 July 1825. Apart from intimating that Ffrench had caused trouble, he stated in it that all had returned to peace and good order, largely because of the prudent conduct of Fr Dollard. Only a few of Ffrench's supporters, he said, the more turbulent ones, had remained disaffected, until he himself, as he put it, "explained your lordship's intention to them with regard to this Monkish Intruder . . . . So, my Lord, I have gained a complete victory over my monkish adversary, who, in truth, since I came here, has made no resistance. His wiles are all discovered and he is now looked on by all classes even by his former warmest friends as an infamous intruder." The claim that McMahon had arranged this peace and that everyone had turned against Ffrench is an instance of fine embroidery, and the admission that Ffrench at no time attempted to assert himself attests to the latter's own peaceable intentions.

---

[35] AAQ NB II no. 74, Dollard to Plessis (Saint John, 9 June 1825).
[36] AAQ NB II no. 75, Dollard to Plessis (Fredericton, 22 June 1825).

Ch. 6. Discoveries and Disappointments   109

McMahon had brought with him a suspension for Ffrench, but it was left to his judgement whether or not to impose it. He never did so. The archbishop's directions to McMahon were as follows: "You will prudently turn away your parishioners, by insinuation rather than by public warning, from any spiritual relation with Mr Charles Ffrench, and if he continues to celebrate mass or to do any other ecclesiastical function, you will indicate to him, in the presence of two witnesses, of the suspension enclosed herewith, so that the people are no longer led astray by this vagabond religious. But before indicating it to him you will ascertain if it is true that he has exercised all the functions that it mentions." McMahon showed the suspension to Ffrench, in the presence of Dollard, but did not deliver it, presumably because Ffrench had not, in fact, been exercising all the functions it mentioned or administering the sacraments except *in articulo mortis*. He then wrote to Plessis, "I have not suspended French, but have expressly told him, in Mr Dollard's presence, that I would certainly deliver it to him, if he should dare to proceed one step further. He promised obedience on the spot, and told us, that he would sooner permit his right arm to be amputated than he should act against your Lordship's authority."[37] The fervour with which Ffrench's assertion was made must have impressed McMahon deeply, for his change of mind about the Dominican began almost at once.

The suspension, written in Latin and in Plessis' hand, bears the date of 28 May 1825.[38] Perhaps the best way to characterize it is to liken it to a conviction grounded on false evidence.

---

[37] AAQ RL XII no. 249, Plessis to McMahon (Quebec, 29 May 1825); AAQ NB II no. 76, McMahon to Plessis (Saint John, 14 July 1825). Dollard's own account of the incident does not differ materially from McMahon's. He reported that, after Ffrench had seen the suspension, "he submitted, and this induced Mr McMahon not to give it to him" (AAQ NB II no. 75, Dollard to Plessis [Fredericton, 22 June 1825]).

[38] AAQ IPE I no. 93 Exemplar, Déclaration de Suspense pour Mr Chs Ffrench (Quebec, 28 May 1825).

Consider the premises upon which it is based, the first of which is that Ffrench had come without a testimonial from Bishop Connolly. It was indeed true that Ffrench did not return with a formal exeat in his possession, for he had lost most of his papers, including Connolly's testimonial, en route to New Brunswick, when he was ship-wrecked off New England.[39] However, he was certainly in possession of an exeat later, for Bishop Fenwick would refer to it in his Memoranda.[40] Moreover, since Connolly had worked with Ffrench for four years on the most delicate issues and had not written one word to his detriment, it is inconceivable that he would not give him the very strongest of recommendations. Plessis himself had written to Cardinal Fontana that Connolly placed confidence in Ffrench and continued to prefer him to the rest of his clergy. Finally, Bishop Connolly had sent testimonials for Ffrench to Quebec on 18 January 1822, along with Ffrench's own request to Plessis for faculties.

The charge that Ffrench, on the pretext of having been elected missionary and pastor of St. Malachy's, had administered the sacraments, is refuted by Ffrench's own letter of 2 December 1824 to the Saint John congregation, in which he explained that he could accept its offer to have him as pastor only if he had authority from his bishop to do so. This response, as well as the proceedings of the meeting of the congregation at which the offer was made, were published in the *City Gazette* of 2 December and the *New-Brunswick Courier* of 11 December 1824.[41] Since no suspension had ever been imposed, Ffrench's offering mass and reading the epistle and gospel had not transgressed Plessis' prohibition of 1817. Nor is there any evidence that he had administered the sacraments save that of

---

[39] *A Short Memoir*, 5.

[40] AAB, Memoranda of the Diocese of Boston [Memoranda], 24 Nov. 1826.

[41] SCAR, Charles Ffrench dossier, doc. 2 (*City Gazette*, 2 Dec. 1824) and doc. 3 (*New-Brunswick Courier*, 11 Dec. 1824).

penance to those *in articulo mortis*, which is allowed any priest, whether in good or in bad standing.

For his part, however, Plessis had not been slow in appealing to higher authority to bolster his conviction of the Dominican, for scarcely a week after writing out the suspension he had submitted to the Prefect of Propaganda, Cardinal Giulio Somaglia, an outline of what he believed to be the facts about Ffrench's behaviour. In his report he charged Ffrench with installing himself as parish priest without diocesan approval. No reply to this letter, which, of course, was based on inaccurate or misinterpreted reports, has been found.[42]

It is clear that McMahon quickly changed his mind about Ffrench. In early October 1825, less than three months after his arrival in Saint John, Fr McMahon wrote one of the most courageous letters ever sent to Plessis by a subordinate. So much so, that it deserves to be extensively quoted:

> As to the desire, which your Lordship seems to express of ascertaining whether Ffrench has heard (extra casum necessitatis) any confessions or not, I can safely say, from what I have been able to learn, on that, as well as on other points, that he has never committed himself in any one manner whatsoever, except in saying Mass and preaching the word of God. The poor unfortunate fellow conducts himself very becomingly towards me, and from what I have been able to gather from the different quarters in [which] he has been most talked of, I think that, in many things, he is an injured man. I cannot help, my Lord, remarking that I feel a secret regard for him, on acct of his firm attachment to the Catholic Church, particularly when I consider how very advantageously, temporally speaking, he might have apostatized in this anti-catholic province where he would not fail to meet with the most flattering encouragements from the first down to the meanest man

---

[42] APF LDNA vol. 2 (1792-1830) pt. 3, 408-411, Plessis to Somaglia (Quebec, 7 June 1825).

in the province; from the Governour to the lowest of *his blue-nosed* subjects. I think, then, my Lord, that he should not be hunted down like a wild beast, but, on the contrary, be treated with a *little* kindness.[43]

Manifestly, then, McMahon had radically altered his opinion of Ffrench, and must have been persuaded to do so, not only by the favorable testimony of the Saint John populace, but also by the conduct and demeanor of Ffrench himself.

Plessis had little chance to think about McMahon's letter for, in the early days of December 1825, he was called to his just reward and his mitre inherited by his auxiliary, Bernard Claude Panet. McMahon did not give up his new championship of Charles Ffrench. His letter of 17 July 1826 to Panet contained another plea for the Dominican: "Poor Ffrench conducts himself well, I hope your Lordship will have pity on him." Panet, however, was as pitiless as his predecessor, for he refused ever to re-consider Ffrench's case. In fact, his reply to McMahon was categorical: "I will not deviate from the path that my predecessor traced for me. So much the better for him [Ffrench] if he is behaving well."[44]

In fact, Plessis' harsh and intractable stance towards Ffrench was seconded by all save one of his successor bishops. The sole exception to this pattern appears to have been Bishop Angus MacEachern of Charlottetown who, after reading the newspaper account of the meeting at which the Saint John congregation expressed its hope to have Ffrench named as pastor in the spring of 1825, had written to Archbishop Plessis in the following terms: "I wrote on the 14th of said month [April] to the chairman, telling him in terms very unequivocal that Mr French should never be received as missionary within the

---

[43] AAQ NB II no. 77, McMahon to Plessis (Saint John, 4 Oct. 1825).

[44] AAQ NB II no. 82, McMahon to Panet (Saint John, 17 July 1826); AAQ RL XII no. 503, Panet to McMahon (Quebec, 3 Aug. 1826).

Diocese, and telling our people to have nothing to do with him. And that, perhaps, the chairman was not ignorant of the *causes*." Yet two years later he would write to Bishop Panet as follows: "I am clearly of opinion that he [Ffrench] should be employed in this diocese." Then he would add, as if in explanation, "I was at Miramichi etc."[45] Two inferences can be adduced from these last statements. First, they would probably not have been made had Archbishop Plessis still been alive, since MacEachern knew very well what Plessis' position on the matter would have been. Furthermore, MacEachern might have had no compunction in speaking his piece to a superior who never once visited the more easterly reaches of his diocese. Indeed, his words, "I was at Miramichi etc." imply that his own experience of the territory and its people should be sufficient to influence Panet's uninformed opinion. Thus it may be argued that MacEachern had come to the conclusion that Ffrench's actual misconduct, if any, was not such as to merit the sort of sanctions imposed by Plessis. It may be also that MacEachern's sacerdotal requirements were sufficiently pressing as to make the risk of Bishop Panet's displeasure worth the challenge: in another letter of the same date, addressed to his friend Paul MacPherson of the Scots College in Rome, MacEachern claimed that Quebec did nothing to alleviate his shortage of priests, and that monies available for sustaining priestly candidates during their seminary years went more often than not to those who were destined for established parishes rather than to those who would probably be assigned to the mission stations.[46]

But Panet was adamant in re-affirming his position. "Never fear that Mr Ffrench will be employed in the diocese, at least during my lifetime," he replied. "His conduct at Miramichi is too well known."[47]

---

[45] AAQ IPE I no. 92, MacEachern to Plessis (St. Andrew's, 2 May 1825); ADC, MacEachern to Panet (St. Andrew's, 6 May 1827).
[46] ADC, MacEachern to MacPherson (St. Andrew's, 6 May 1827).
[47] AAQ RL XIII no. 198, Panet to MacEachern (Quebec, 7 June 1827).

The result of such continued inaction by the prelates of the diocese was that an investigation into the question of whether Ffrench was actually guilty or innocent of the charges raised against him in New Brunswick was never once initiated after Plessis received, and quickly reacted to, Fr Morisset's original report of the first rumour in the spring of 1817. As a consequence, long decades after the disappearance of the several actors in the drama, the memory of Fr Ffrench's career on the Miramichi was still alive, but riven with error, misinterpretation and exaggeration.[48]

---

[48] See, for example, AAQ NE V no. 166, Placide Gaudet to Henri Têtu (Ottawa, 23 Sept. 1903). We shall refer to this document at greater length in Chapter 9 of this study.

Chapter 7

FINAL PROJECTS:
NEW ENGLAND, ROME, NEW BRUNSWICK
(1826-1851)

By this time, Ffrench had clearly come to the conclusion that he could not expect justice in the Diocese of Quebec. At the end of October 1826, McMahon informed Panet as follows: "Mr Ffrench has left Saint John to go and live in the United States. He hopes the Bishop of Boston will do something for him."[1] That Ffrench was cordially received and taken on by Bishop Benedict Fenwick was, in no small measure, the product of McMahon's own intervention. Unbeknownst to Panet, he wrote a highly commendatory letter about Ffrench to Bishop Fenwick. Doubtless, too, Fenwick already knew of Ffrench's excellent work for Bishop Connolly in New York. He had, after all, preceded him as pastor at Old St. Peter's. In any event, the Bishop of Boston was pleased to obtain Ffrench's services, for, as he wrote in his Memoranda:

> Mr Ffrench arrives from St. Johns. He brings with him an Exeat from the Right Revd Doctor Connolly, late Bishop of New York where he was last employed, and a very strong recommendation from the Revd McMahon, the pastor at St. Johns, near whom he lived this sometime past, without being in any manner engaged in the ministry. The testimony of the last mentioned Revd Gentleman in regard to the character of the Revd Ffrench since his

---

[1] AAQ NB II no. 87, McMahon to Panet (Saint John, 31 Oct. 1826).

acquaintence with him at St. Johns is highly gratifying.²

On the strength of these papers, Fenwick gave Ffrench faculties and stationed him at Eastport, Maine, recommending that he build, if possible, a church there and attend especially to the Passamaquoddy Indians near that town. After receiving his commission from Fenwick, Ffrench thanked McMahon for his help and described the friendly reception he had received at Fenwick's hands. He did not, of course, neglect to mention his new assignment at Eastport, which lay on the Maine-New Brunswick border. Fenwick's commission as Vicar-General of the Diocese of Quebec for those parts of New Brunswick adjoining Maine were, in turn, imparted to Ffrench, who for the previous four years had been persistently refused those very faculties by the bishops of Quebec. The irony of Ffrench's appointment cannot have been lost on any of the parties involved. Certainly it was not lost on McMahon, who reported the event to Panet in the following terms:

> Mr Ffrench has been appointed by the Bishop of Boston to a mission called East-Port; it is in the vicinity of St. Andrew's. He says that the Bishop of Boston, as your Vicar General, has given him faculties to officiate *en passant* in this part of your diocese; despite that, I have forbidden him to do that in my district until I receive a letter from your Lordship. Can he then, by virtue of the powers of Monseignor of Boston exercise his ministry with respect to those of Your subjects who are on the borders of your diocese? Can he say Mass or preach in the church of Saint John, when he comes here on a visit? Can he render spiritual services to the Catholics of St. Andrew's and neighbourhood? He told me that the Bishop of Boston gave him that power. . . . East-Port, where Mr Ffrench is located, is 25 leagues from

---

² AAB Memoranda, 24 Nov. 1826.

here. It is in the diocese of Boston and in the United States.³

Panet once more refused Ffrench permission to officiate in his diocese, even on its boundaries.⁴ Bishop Fenwick, on the other hand, like most clerics in the eastern colonies and states, knew all about the charges laid to Ffrench's account, so that his reception of the Dominican into his diocese shows unequivocally that he did not believe them. Indeed, his choice of posting at Eastport is a subtle manifestation of his belief in Ffrench's innocence.

Ffrench's new mission was even more extensive than the one he had served along the shores of the Miramichi. It embraced, in the southeast, all of the seaboard districts from Portland to Eastport, and included portions of southeastern New Hampshire and northeastern Massachusetts. Over the next dozen years, he replicated, in his new district, his church-building achievements in the old. In 1827 he began construction of St. Joseph's at Eastport. By 1828, St. Aloysius' at Dover and St. Dominic's at Portland were "in a state of forwardness" or "progressing fast." All three were of brick. Ffrench built only one other church, at Lawrence, Massachusetts, in 1847, near the end of his ministry.⁵ Records also make it clear that he was active among the Indians living around the Passamoquoddy and that communicants residing at St. Andrew's, in New Brunswick, crossed over to Eastport for confirmation by Bishop Fenwick.⁶ For a dozen years (1826-1838) Ffrench was occupied with the stations of his extensive missions. Concurrently he was a

---

³ AAQ NB II no. 88, McMahon to Panet (Saint John, 12 Dec. 1826).
⁴ AAQ RL XIII no. 116, Panet to McMahon (Quebec, 18 Jan. 1827). See also AAQ RL XIII no. 154, Panet to MacEachern (Quebec, 30 March 1827).
⁵ AAB Memoranda, 24 Aug. 1826; 1 Aug. 1828; 10 Nov. 1846.
⁶ AAB Memoranda, 19 July 1827.

frequent visitor to Boston, where, more often than not, he raised funds for his several churches.

By 1838, Ffrench seems to have decided that the progress and the accomplishments he had made in his charge were sufficiently advanced that he could entertain the prospect of a visit to Ireland. In anticipation of such a journey he sent a report of the financial situation of his Portland congregation to Bishop Fenwick on 17 May of that year. Passing through Portland on his way back to Boston from one of his outlying missions the following October, Fenwick stopped and stayed a few days with Ffrench, writing in the Memoranda that he had "examined the accounts of the Rev. Mr. Ffrench about to return to Europe" and had found them to be accurate and satisfactory. A week later Fenwick appointed a Fr Simon Flood "to take Rev. F. Ffrench's place who has resigned his situation with the view of proceeding to Ireland." At the end of another fortnight, having introduced Fr Flood to his new parishioners, Ffrench was in Boston preparing to leave for Europe via New York. On the day of his departure for New York, he submitted his accounts with the Congregation of Portland, which concluded, "On examination it appears that a balance of $3000 is due him from [us]." This debt, it was agreed, was to be liquidated from the Surplus Fund of the congregation over a period of years.[7]

When and where Ffrench arrived in Ireland or how long he remained there is now impossible to establish. One can assume, nevertheless, that he visited relatives and friends and renewed acquaintanceship with his old haunts. The first written evidence of his European sojourn is dated from Rome on 26 April 1840. This document, a 38-page memoir written in longhand and titled "The Conversion of Charles Ffrench to the Catholic Church," has already been cited more than once in this study. Its preface tells us that he was solicited by "a very respectable personage" to

---

[7] AAB Memoranda, 17 May 1838; 21, 26 and 30 Oct. 1838; 6 Nov. 1838.

write the particulars of his conversion and the beneficial effects of his ministry. About two-thirds of the work encompasses Ffrench's early life and education to 1801, or until his return to Ireland from Portugal. The remainder scans his career as a missionary and the problems, hardships, and obstacles he met with in New Brunswick, New England, and New York. The document is striking in that it not once mentions either Ffrench's differences with Fr Malou or what he considered his unjust treatment at the hands of Archbishop Plessis. In fact, it mentions no specific controversies at all.[8]

In addition to these pursuits, Ffrench embraced the opportunity to pursue what was perhaps his most cherished ambition, the establishment of a Dominican college at Saint John. His principal steps in that direction were petitions to the Secretary of Propaganda (28 April 1840), to the Master General of the Dominican Order (14 June 1840), and to the Supreme Pontiff, Gregory XVI (28 July 1840). After examination and recommendation by Propaganda, the request was granted, with two conditions: first, the proposed college must be given a constitution and organization modelled on that of the College of Corpo Santo in Lisbon and, secondly, the Ordinary of the diocese in which it was erected must give his approval. His request to Propaganda also asked for special functions, namely, to bless rosaries, to erect stations of the cross, and to establish confraternities of the scapular, but no decision as to whether or not these were received has been found.[9] The next phase of Ffrench's campaign was set into motion when, on 18 July 1840, the Prefect of Propaganda, Cardinal Giacomo Filippo Fransoni, very likely at Ffrench's insistence, penned the strongest of

---

[8] SCAR, Charles Ffrench dossier, file 28, doc. 62a. See Appendix B for complete text.

[9] APF UNS vol. 92 fols. 538r-539v, 540r-541v, 542r-543v; APF LDNA vol. 4 (1837-1841) pt. 2, fols. 419r-419v ["Petition"]. A translation of the Italian text of Ffrench's petition to Pope Gregory XVI comprises Appendix C of this study.

recommendations to Bishop Bernard Donald Macdonald of Charlottetown in favour of the college.[10]

Ffrench's petition to the Holy Father recommended that a second Vicariate Apostolic be erected over the twelfth district of Nova Scotia and that the administration of the new vicariate be committed to the Dominicans. According to Ffrench, the spiritual needs of the province justified such a move, for it embraced an area more than half the size of Italy, an area which its present vicar apostolic—whose seat at Antigonish was over 200 miles distant—could rarely visit to administer the sacraments. In the meantime the Catholic population in the region had expanded considerably, through natural increase, through increments from among the Loyalist settlers, and latterly by the arrival of the Irish. A second vicariate was therefore warranted, Ffrench maintained. The document also makes mention of the fact that permission to establish a Dominican college had already been granted.[11]

It has been suggested that the location and the extent of the "twelfth district" referred to in the petition to Pope Gregory XVI coincided with three of the Fundyside counties, namely Kings, Annapolis and Digby, together with the two most southerly shires, Yarmouth and Shelburne.[12] It is reasonable indeed to conclude that the modern diocese of Yarmouth is underpinned by, and encompasses, this proposed vicariate, whose surface area would have covered some 4,795 square miles and would have been upwards of 200 miles in length. Ffrench was not exaggerating the magnitude of the problems endured by the Catholics in the western reaches of the province. Until the arrival of Fr Jean-Mandé Sigogne in the mission in mid-June of 1799, the dispersed and dispirited Catholics, former Acadian exiles for

---

[10] *St. Andrew's Chronicle*, 12 March 1841, quoting *Saint John Chronicle*.
[11] "Petition."
[12] Angus Anthony Johnston, *A History of the Catholic Church in Eastern Nova Scotia*, 2 vols. (Antigonish: St. Francis Xavier University Press, 1960-1971), vol. 1, 174-175.

the most part, had been attended to by a number of transient clergy. For the four decades following his arrival, Fr Sigogne worked among his flock quietly and unfalteringly, with but infrequent assistance. By the time Ffrench composed his petition for an additional vicariate, Sigogne was seventy-seven years of age, truly ancient by the missionary standards of the time, fifty-three of which he spent in the priesthood. During that time, this "apostle of the Acadians" constructed seven churches, one of which, at Bear River, was assigned to the Mi'kmaqs. From about 1835 on, the old missionary was plagued with an increasing paralysis which ultimately required that he have assistance when taking even the shortest of walks.[13] Clearly some decisive action was required to preserve a mission so in need of attention.

On more than one occasion, we have noted the hearty and constant feelings that Ffrench and the population of Saint John, both Catholic and Protestant, entertained for one another. Whether far away in the American states or nearby along the Miramichi, Ffrench maintained a frequent if irregular contact with several of his old parishioners. Doubtless, too, he, as well as the resident missionaries in Saint John after him, knew their counterpart on the opposite shores quite well. The financial arrangements entered into between Frs McQuade and Sigogne in 1818 had amply demonstrated that fact. The brisk and steady commercial and mercantile trade carried on between Saint John and the outports of the Nova Scotian shore likewise assisted the interchange of news and views, ecclesiastical as well as civil. For instance, Fr Sigogne informed Morisset of cases of the thievery of chattels, as also of the pitiful situation of the Indian population of his mission.[14] It is not surprising, therefore, that Ffrench was relatively well acquainted with the critical state of the church along the south-western shores. Moreover, his vision of an

---

[13] Bernard Pothier, "Sigogne, Jean-Mandé," *Dictionary of Canadian Biography* VII (1836-1850), 800-806; Guy Léger, "L'Eglise de Yarmouth fête ses noces d'argent," *L'Eglise canadienne* 11 (1 June 1978), 601-603.

[14] AAQ NB II no. 41, Morisset to Plessis (Saint John, 6 Nov. 1822).

additional vicariate included, not surprisingly, the proposed college at Saint John, to which students could be sent to be ordained.[15]

A nine-page document discovered in the Propaganda Archives and apparently written in Ffrench's own hand is almost certainly related to this project. Although undated, it appears to have been written in Rome at the time of Ffrench's visit there and it bears the title "Details sur la province de Nouvelle Brunswick." In it, Ffrench divides his subject into three sections: a northern district embracing the Miramichi area, a middle district centred on Fredericton, and a southern district dominated by Saint John. Within each district he identifies the principal population centres, the chief geographical features, and the number and placement of the churches. He also offers a brief assessment of the twelfth district's suitability as a vicariate.[16]

To the researcher, the discovery of Ffrench's proposal for the establishment of a second vicariate comes like a bolt from the blue. There is no evidence, either material or oral, as to how or when the idea germinated, and as far as can be ascertained no response to it has ever been found. On the other hand, several documents in Rome, Charlottetown, and Saint John do address the subject of a new Dominican college.

Ffrench wasted no time in leaving Rome and it is clear that, once in New York, he wrote to Bishop Macdonald to inform him of the permission he had received for the founding of a college at Saint John, in pursuance of which he requested faculties in the diocese. Macdonald's response was as negative and as adamant as those of Plessis and Panet had been in earlier years. Notwithstanding the support Ffrench had been given by Cardinal

---

[15] "Petition."
[16] Two different copies of this document, both apparently in Ffrench's handwriting, have been discovered, but one of them is slightly abridged. The longer copy comprises Appendix D of this study. The shorter copy can be found in APF LDNA vol. 4 (1837-1841) pt. 3, 517-525.

Fransoni, the reply he received from Charlottetown ended as follows: "He [Macdonald] therefore hopes that you will not put yourself to any trouble or expense in the city of St. John in the vain hope of receiving on some future day faculties which the respect due to the memory of his illustrious predecessors, as well as the peace of his conscience compell him to refuse." Bishop Macdonald did not answer Ffrench directly, but communicated through his secretary. This practice stands in stark contrast to Macdonald's correspondence with Fr Dollard for, on the very day on which his secretary replied to Ffrench, Macdonald wrote personally to Dollard telling him of Ffrench's request and his rejection of it. Indeed, he assumed that Dollard understood and concurred fully with his reasoning, since he wrote, "It is unnecessary for me to say for your information that I consider it my duty prudently to use every means religion will allow to prevent his ever officiating in any Clerical Capacity in the Diocese." He also informed Dollard that he had written to Propaganda "complaining in respectful but strong terms of the manner in which those faculties have been given him [Ffrench], & requesting them to be withdrawn." No reply from Rome has been found. Macdonald went even further, for he asked Dollard to inform Fr James Dunphy, then the incumbent at St. Malachy's, of Ffrench's request and its fate, the bishop all the while assuring Dollard, "Mr Dunphy will, I have no doubt, continue to discountenance the Rev'd. gentleman and treat him in the manner which his well meditated & intended intrusion deserves."[17]

Despite Macdonald's letter, Fr Ffrench left New York for Saint John, no doubt confident that the documents he had received from Rome would eventually prevail. However, as a result of the bishop's directive, Fr Dunphy announced to his parishioners at Sunday mass that Ffrench was not authorized to

---

[17] ADC, R. Lafrance to Ffrench (Charlottetown, 4 Jan. 1841); ADC, Macdonald to Dollard (Rustico, 4 Jan. 1841).

officiate in the diocese and he forbade them to attend mass and vespers if Fr Ffrench attempted to do so. On the other hand, the congregation supported Fr Ffrench. It was already at odds with Fr Dunphy over other of his actions, policies, and language, and it raised vehement objections to his remarks, especially to the assertions of his partisans that Ffrench's documents were forgeries. Ffrench's supporters then appealed to the expertise of a Latin scholar, Mr James Patterson, the principal of the Saint John Grammar School. After examining for authenticity the documents and papers in Fr Ffrench's possession, Patterson reported that both they and the seals accompanying them were valid. Three documents were authenticated. The first was a grant from His Holiness, Gregory XVI, to Fr Ffrench to establish a college in Saint John, which would be placed under the auspices of the Propaganda Fide and the Bishop of Charlottetown, with the same privileges that had been granted to the College of Corpo Santo in Lisbon. The second was a licence granted by the pontiff to Fr Ffrench to celebrate mass throughout New Brunswick, among other privileges. The third was a letter from Cardinal Fransoni, Prefect of Propaganda, to the Right Reverend Bernard Donald Macdonald, Bishop of Charlottetown, in which he recommended Ffrench "again and again in the strongest terms." The undertaking Ffrench had begun, the Cardinal asserted, would be very useful in religion and "it was highly approved of by the Sacred Congregation. I trust you will afford him every assistance and co-operation in your power to further the laudable institution."[18]

And, of course, records in the Vatican indicate that the documents were indeed valid.

The publication in the local newspaper of Mr Patterson's judgement and the content of the documents gave considerable satisfaction to Ffrench, for it removed from the minds of the New Brunswick community all doubt about the authenticity of

---

[18] *St. Andrew's Chronicle*, 12 March 1841, quoting *Saint John Chronicle*.

his proposal. He took the occasion gently to reprove Fr Dunphy for his distorted view, which had been the source of so much anxiety and scandal. In addition, the opposition to Ffrench by the pastor and the bishop prompted a number of the St. Malachy's congregation to request the Reverend Fr La Marche at the Minerva in Rome to translate into Italian a petition of their own to the Holy Father. The gist of their petition was that the pontiff should appoint Fr Ffrench to be pastor at St. Malachy's. Appended to it was a certificate signed by the town major, John Gallagher, testifying to the esteem and high standing in which the Protestant community of Saint John held Fr Ffrench as well. No response to this petition has been located.[19]

Eventually, however, Fr Ffrench realized that he was not going to be able to execute his plan, episcopal permission having been denied, and he left Saint John. The Fenwick Memoranda record that he reached Boston on 15 June 1842. They further relate that Ffrench "has, since his return from Europe, resided at St. John's New Brunswick where he contemplated erecting a Dominican convent to which Order he belongs–but it seems he has entirely abandoned the idea." According to the same source, Ffrench then expressed the wish that he be received once again into the Diocese of Boston.[20]

Fr Charles Dominic Ffrench died in Lawrence, Massachusetts, on 5 Jan. 1851. Analysis of his missionary life in New England after 1827 is beyond the scope of this study.[21]

---

[19] APF LDNA vol. 4 (1837-1841) pt. 3, fols. 533r-534v, Henry McCullough et al. to Fr La Marche (Saint John, 27 Feb. 1841); fols. 539r-540r, John Gallagher to Propaganda (Saint John, 1841); fols. 541r-542v, Henry McCullough et al. to Pope Gregory XVI (Saint John, 27 Feb. 1841); *St. Andrew's Chronicle*, 12 March 1841, quoting *Saint John Chronicle*.

[20] AAB Memoranda, 15 June 1842.

[21] For details on Ffrench's activities after his final return to the United States, see O'Daniel's unpublished manuscript, "Appendix E," 220-234. Most of O'Daniel's summary is gleaned from the Memoranda

Suffice to say that his reputation in his new territory remained unsullied. Indeed, Archbishop Michael Augustine Corrigan of New York, who later examined Ffrench's career, concluded that the Dominican had been thoroughly vindicated in an unpublished manuscript written by the well-known author and poet, Margaret E. Jordan.[22] It is certainly clear that the four American ordinaries under whom Ffrench served–John Connolly, Benedict Fenwick, John Hughes, and Bernard Fitzpatrick–thought very highly of him. Writing in the Boston Diocese Memoranda after Ffrench's death, Bishop Fitzpatrick seems to have summed up the feelings of all:

> He [Ffrench] was a man of great bodily beauty and magnificent personal appearance–tall and, although weighing three hundred and fifty pounds, not disproportionate in [any] way, nor unwieldy. In the ministry he was remarkable for his zeal, energy and enterprise, and the piety of his conduct and regularity of life. His manners were most amiable and winning; his temper even and placid; his spirits buoyant and sprightly, though seasoned with becoming gravity. Perhaps the most remarkable of his virtues was the charity which regulated at all times his conversation. He was never heard to speak ill of any person, and the ingenuity with which he would endeavour to

---

and local newspapers. See also William Lucey S.J., "Charles Ffrench and the Maine Coast," in *The Catholic Church in Maine* (Francistown, N.H.: Marshall Jones & Co., 1952), 65-81.

[22] *Historical Records and Studies* 2 (1901), 40-42. *Register of Clergy*. Ffrench, Rev. Charles Dominic, O.S.D. Victor O'Daniel writes that he contacted Margaret Jordan but that she refused to let him see the manuscript, saying that she wanted to use it herself ("Appendix E," 241-242n.60). We found no evidence that she did so, nor had we any success in locating the manuscript itself.

Over a hundred years ago, William Leahy termed Ffrench an exemplary early American missionary in the Boston area (William Byrne et al., *History of the Catholic Church in the New England States*, 2 vols. [Boston: Hurd & Everts, 1899], vol. 1, 42).

> present in some favourable light the faults even of his own enemies was at times as amusing as it was edifying.[23]

Even allowing for the fact that it is natural to refer to a recently deceased person in a charitable way, a declaration such as Bishop Fitzpatrick's is not made with private reservations. In the face of this and other such favorable assessments and in the absence of any firm evidence of Fr Ffrench's alleged misconduct other than malicious rumours, confessed lies, and suspect testimony, it is difficult to understand how his reputation has continued for so long to remain grounded in the wilfulness of some to believe the worst.

---

[23] AAB Memoranda, 7 Jan. 1851. O'Daniel, who examined the Memoranda carefully, states that they contain nothing but praise of Ffrench ("Appendix E," 197).

Old St. Peter's Church, New York, 1785.
Courtesy Rev. Kevin V. Madigan, New York, N.Y.

Chapter 8

THE ROLE OF NATIONALISM IN THE CASE AGAINST FR FFRENCH

Any discussion of nationalism in a particular controversy is bound to be a thorny one, yet there is no doubt that national bias played a role in Fr Ffrench's fortunes, both in Canada and in the United States. The degree of and the reasons for this role are, however, much more difficult to assess than its actual presence. Some writers analyzing events affecting Fr Ffrench have commented on the subject without treating its role in depth, while others have dismissed or ignored the issue. A few have published cogent and useful remarks on the subject.[1] Despite the

---

[1] Those publications that we have found particularly useful in the context of this chapter are John Jennings, *Tending the Flock: Bishop Joseph-Octave Plessis and Roman Catholics in Early 19th Century New Brunswick* (Saint John: Diocese of Saint John, 1998); Luca Codignola, "The Policy of Rome towards the English-Speaking Catholics in British North America, 1750-1830" ["The Policy of Rome"], in Terrence Murphy and Gerald Stortz, eds., *Creed and Culture: The Place of English-Speaking Catholics in Canadian Society, 1750-1930* [*Creed and Culture*] (Montreal & Kingston: McGill-Queen's University Press, 1993), 100-125; Terrence Murphy, "Trusteeism in Atlantic Canada: The Struggle for Leadership among the Irish Catholics of Halifax, St. John's, and Saint John, 1780-1850" ["Trusteeism in Atlantic Canada"], also in *Creed and Culture*, 126-151; Allan MacDonald, "Angus Bernard MacEachern, 1759-1835: His Ministry in the Maritime Provinces," in Terrence Murphy and Cyril J. Byrne, eds., *Religion and Identity: The Experience of Irish and Scottish Catholics in Atlantic Canada* (St. John's: Jesperson Press, 1987), 53-67; Ronnie Gilles LeBlanc, "Antoine Gagnon and the Mitre: A Model of Relations Between *Canadien*, Scottish and Irish Clergy in the Early

obvious hazards, this chapter shall attempt to identify the ways in which nationalism negatively affected Fr Ffrench's career. The extent to which blame can be assigned in the operation of this factor is left to the reader to judge.

Since the saga of Fr Ffrench in North America began essentially with the period during which he worked as a missionary under Archbishop Plessis, it is to the question of bias in Quebec and New Brunswick that we shall turn first, in an attempt to analyze Ffrench's relations with Plessis himself, and to a lesser extent his fellow-missionaries and congregation. Then, after an examination of the way in which a destructive nationalism played a part in events in New York, a brief assessment can be made of the way in which the two currents further combined to help prevent justice from functioning in Ffrench's favour.

In 1852, the year after Ffrench's death, Charles Etienne Brasseur de Bourbourg published in Paris an overview of impressions he had received while on a visit to North America. His remarks are especially *à propos* here, in particular those he made on the origins and evolution of the reciprocal antipathy of the Irish and the *Canadiens*. Bourbourg began with the assertion that the Catholic charity of the *Canadien* clergy and people had been liberally extended to the waves of Irish immigrants arriving on Quebec shores during the first decades of the nineteenth century. Whilst they were so engaged, "the national character, more than once getting the upper hand," had given rise, among the *Canadiens*, to a "jealous defiance of the proliferation of these foreigners whom they saw imperceptibly establish themselves among them and take a place in the country." Though subjects of

---

Maritime Church," also in *Religion and Identity*, 98-113; Luca Codignola, "Conflict or Consensus? Catholics in Canada and in the United States, 1780-1820" ["Conflict or Consensus"], CCHA *Historical Studies* 55 (1988), 43-59; and Ronin Murther, "The Life of the Most Reverend Ambrose Maréchal Third Archbishop of Baltimore, 1768-1828" ["Ambrose Maréchal"], Ph.D. thesis, Catholic University of America, 1965.

Ch. 8. The Role of Nationalism in the Case 131

England, the *Canadiens* neither liked the English nor those who spoke English. Furthermore, for most of them, to be *Canadien* and to be Catholic were nearly synonymous; consequently "to learn the language of the conqueror was tantamount to heresy." Bourbourg reasoned that had the Irish adopted the French language they would have fused easily with the *Canadiens*. As it was, they formed a Catholic people, a people who lived in the midst of the *Canadiens* but who spoke a language that was repugnant to their hosts. In time, the rapid expansion of Irish numbers transformed the jealous defiance of the *Canadiens* into a fear that they would eventually be outnumbered and absorbed; this was a prospect that would be abetted by their mutual adherence to a common religion and a common law.

According to Brasseur de Bourbourg, the establishment of St. Patrick's Church in Quebec City, constructed during Archbishop Panet's episcopate (1825-1833), externalized these fears and apprehensions. An old Recollet church having been lent to the Irish of Montreal by the more liberal *Canadien* clergy and fabric of that city during Archbishop Plessis' reign, their compatriots in Quebec City had requested the same or a similar concession on numerous occasions. To no avail. The parish priest of Quebec and coadjutor of the Diocese, Rev. Joseph Signaÿ, and the fabricants were as one in their opposition to Irish supplications. Nor had Archbishop Plessis encouraged them. Affairs had continued to run along with nothing achieved until the return of Fr Patrick McMahon from Saint John in 1828. After taking advantage of the divisions within the fabric council, using the public press to show the intolerance of the fabricants, acquiring the site for a church, suffering a harsh rejection at the hands of the coadjutor, and making a direct plea to Archbishop Panet, McMahon won out. Nevertheless, Signaÿ remained indifferent to the project, if not hostile. When the church was finally completed, Signaÿ, who would succeed Panet in the archiepiscopal seat in 1833, was asked to bless the new temple but absented himself from the city on the appointed date. Resort was subsequently had to the vicar-general of the diocese, Fr

Jérôme Demers, to perform the ritual. Brasseur de Bourbourg claimed that during the thirteen years leading up to the time he himself was writing that section of his book in March 1846, Monseigneur Signaÿ had not visited Saint Patrick's church on a single occasion, even though "it was in the middle of his episcopal city, in which twelve to fourteen thousand Irish were part of his flock."[2]

---

[2] Charles Etienne Brasseur de Bourbourg, *Histoire du Canada, de son église et de ses missions*, 2 vols. (Paris: Sagnier et Bray, 1852; reprint: East Ardsley, Wakefield: S.R. Pubs, 1968), vol. 2, 194-204. For an account of the building of St. Patrick's, see Marianna O'Gallagher S.C.H., *Saint Patrick's, Quebec: The Building of a Church and of a Parish 1827 to 1833* (Quebec: Carraig Books, 1981). O'Gallagher writes that the congregation had petitioned Plessis for an English-speaking priest as early as 1817 and possibly even in 1812, partly in the following terms: "Wherefore your petitioners request that your Lordship will be pleased to nominate the Reverend Charles Ffrench now in the City of Quebec, to officiate for your petitioners as a further encouragement for the Labours of the Reverend Charles Ffrench, promise to subscribe such sums as are specified and affixed here-unto and your Lordship's compliance with their request will make them in duty bound to pray. . ." (33). Of the 53 signatures pledging £135 10s., 42 were Irish. O'Gallagher hesitates to choose between the 1817 date, written in an unknown hand on the letter, and 1812, the year Ffrench arrived in Canada, but 1813 is almost certainly the correct date. For the original letter, see AAQ IQ I no. 100, Inhabitants of Quebec City to Plessis (Quebec, n.d.). It may be this incident to which Ffrench was referring when he wrote in his "Conversion," "My little flock would not hear of my quitting, it was a tryal to me. They were mostly my own converts. They visited in a Body on the Bishop to oblidge me to remain and finding him unwilling to detain me, they were very much dissatisfied" (27-28).

For a summary of the careers of Fr Demers and Bishop Signaÿ, see Claude Galarneau, "Demers, Jérôme," in *Dictionary of Canadian Biography* VIII (1851-1860), 210-215; and Sonia Chassé, "Signay, Joseph," in *Dictionary of Canadian Biography* VII (1836-1850), 798-800.

Such, in any case, were the observations made by Brasseur de Bourbourg with respect to events taking place in Quebec at a time when Fr Ffrench's relations, first with Plessis and then with Panet, were at their most negative.

In his study of the policy of the Vatican towards English-speaking Catholics in North America of the period, Luca Codignola allocates a certain share of the blame for these misunderstandings to Rome itself. As he puts it, "In the mind of the Roman officials, therefore, and indeed of all interested parties in Great Britain, Canada, and the United States, there was no room for debate. The bishop of Quebec was held responsible for French-speaking North Americans, whereas the bishop of Baltimore (or, earlier, the vicar apostolic in the London District) took charge of English speaking North Americans." He indicates that this policy had worked fairly well until after the Seven Years' War, when the Catholics of Canada became British subjects. "At first," he points out, "the bishops of Quebec tried to deal with the Maritimes, where most of the nonfrancophones were, as a simple extension of the St. Lawrence Valley, as if the Canadian Catholic community had not substantially changed after the Conquest," and this became increasingly difficult as immigration expanded. Furthermore, Propaganda was slow to understand that the population was changing in the Maritimes and, because most of its information came from the Quebec hierarchy itself, "the officials of Propaganda were for a long time ill-informed about the new realities of the North American continent and on the needs of its new Catholics."[3] The simple fact that their needs–of which the foremost was, according to many of them, a pastor who could speak their language and who understood their way of thinking–were not being met was

---

[3] Codignola, "The Policy of Rome," 102-108. Codignola's comments on the deficiencies of Propaganda in this respect are echoed by Gerald Fogarty in "Lay Trusteeism: Yesterday and Today" ["Lay Trusteeism"], *America* 115: 21 (19 Nov. 1966), 656-659.

enough to arouse antagonism in many.[4] Indeed, the number of memorials sent by the congregation at Saint John to their bishop at Quebec expressing their desire for a priest of their own culture and language is evidence enough of this factor. And so it should not be surprising that the antagonism became at times reciprocal.

The case of Fr Antoine Gagnon, who was the missionary at Richibucto when Ffrench was at Miramichi and who had been born, raised, and trained in Quebec, is a good illustration of this divergence of views. According to Ronnie Gilles LeBlanc, Gagnon reflected the Quebec perspective to a strong degree and was very anti-British. When Angus MacEachern was appointed auxiliary to the Bishop of Quebec for New Brunswick, Prince Edward Island, Cape Breton and the Îles de la Madeleine, Gagnon "could hardly accept the reality of this first step leading towards separation from the Diocese of Quebec." In fact, "almost four years after Bishop MacEachern's accession, Antoine Gagnon still considered himself as belonging to the Diocese of Quebec but residing in a foreign diocese for the time being." Thus he admitted to a dislike of the Irish and Scots because they did not conform to his way, that is, to the *Québecois* way.[5] Furthermore, Gagnon himself did not speak English, which fact would not have endeared him to the Hibernians, to whom he refers, in a letter to Plessis, as "Irish

---

[4] For instance, oratory, at which Fr Ffrench was proficient, but which was not the most important of a priest's capabilities in the eyes of the *Canadien* episcopate, was highly valued by the Irish. One memorial to Plessis from St. Malachy's stated that Fr Ffrench "has few competitors in the pulpit" (AAQ NB II no. 60 [Saint John, 15 Dec. 1824]). And Fr Morisset complained about the parishioners at St. Andrew's, who were in the process of building a church but did not have a priest of their own. "One of them," he wrote, "told me, I suppose in the name of all the others, that he would not give a cent for a priest unless he was a powerful orator" (AAQ NB II no. 40, Morisset to Plessis [Saint John, 6 Oct. 1822]).

[5] LeBlanc, "Antoine Gagnon and the Mitre," 101-103.

ragamuffins."⁶ LeBlanc explains, "The main obstacle in his [Gagnon's] relations with priests of backgrounds other than French or *Quebécois*, was their particular views or conceptions of ecclesiastical discipline, views that differed from his own," and he states that in this attitude Gagnon was well supported by the Bishops of Quebec, including Plessis.⁷ Small wonder, then, that Gagnon was scandalized by Ffrench's neglect of the cassock and his pursuit of donations from the Protestants, and that he considered these things to be matters of importance to convey to his bishop. Ffrench's casual attitude towards finding himself in the company of women other than in an ecclesiastical setting, as well as his willingness to play the violin for their pleasure, would similarly have shocked Gagnon's sensibilities, though such situations would probably have raised few eyebrows in Ireland.

Not that the relations between the Irish and the *Canadiens* were always the ones that were strained. Ffrench himself recognized that there was culture clash in New Brunswick. It was not of the *Canadiens* that he complained, however, but of his fellow English-speakers. "In a mission such as this," he wrote to Plessis from Bartibog, "it is not easy and with a people who give me a general salvo, 'This is not the custom of Scotland.'"⁸ And many years later, Archbishop Panet and Bishop MacEachern would be in agreement that the Irish missionary, John Carroll, should be removed from his mission when he "asserted from the pulpit that he would not serve under any Scotch bishop."⁹ The bishop in question was, of course,

---

⁶ AAQ NB V no. 36, Gagnon to Plessis (Bouctouche, 13 Nov. 1814).
⁷ LeBlanc, "Antoine Gagnon and the Mitre," 101.
⁸ AAQ NB VI no. 143, Ffrench to Plessis (Bartibog, 30 May 1815).
⁹ AAQ IPE I no. 27, MacEachern to Panet (15 Aug. 1832); AAQ RL XV no. 222, Panet to MacEachern (Quebec, Oct. 1832). Terrence Murphy writes that, according to MacEachern, Carroll's actual words were: "Irishmen, look to yourselves, and appoint your own Officers, and do not allow yourselves to be put down by a miserable Scotchman!" ("Trusteeism in Atlantic Canada," 142).

MacEachern himself, who had recently been appointed to the see of Charlottetown, and the mission that of St. Malachy's, which had for so long sought to be served only by Irish clergy.

Plessis' situation was not, of course, a comfortable one. Luca Codignola writes that the Canadian church actually enjoyed more freedom under British rule than it had under that of France and that Plessis had supported Britain in the War of 1812-1814 against the United States.[10] Plessis belonged, nevertheless, to a conquered nation, and even as he cooperated with the British he in no way identified with them. On the other hand, despite their common language the Irish were not the English, and several further factors seem to have conspired to give rise to the anti-Irish sentiments that Plessis himself expresses when writing about them, both clergy and congregations.

Foremost seems to have been the matter of discipline, and not just with respect to small matters. Many of the Irish in the Maritimes were poor and uneducated, as were many of the *Canadiens* for that matter, but the persistence of those whose opinion he could not accept as a reasonable or educated one seems often to have irritated Plessis. The Irish, he found, were not as amenable to suggestion as were the *Canadiens*. Perhaps one of the more moderate manifestations of the bishop's views about the former appears in a letter of 1821 to Fr Joseph Morisset. In it, he assured the latter, "The ignorance of a part of your flock ought to surprise you not at all. It is composed of families of beggars. These types of people are very little concerned with learning Christian doctrine. All their vision is limited to procuring the basic necessities of life, without any other activity than that of exciting in their favour the compassion of the public by the always exaggerated recital of their misery and their powerlessness." He also noted, however, that in their interests and priorities many of the *Canadiens* of the countryside differed little from the lower orders of the Irish. By contrast, he

---

[10] Codignola, "Conflict or Consensus," 53.

pointed out, the Irish of the middle classes who had studied religion knew it much better than the *Canadiens* of the same ranks but were "neither less warm in their ideas nor less turbulent in their enterprises. This comes from the national character."[11] It was, of course, the exuberant expression of this "national character" that irked Plessis the most, and one manifestation of it was the determination of the Saint John congregation to have a say in choosing its own priest. The many petitions for Ffrench to be pastor there will thus have served simply to settle Plessis all the more firmly in his opinion, especially as he was not accustomed to having his authority as an archbishop ignored. No doubt even the indifference of many to the idea of attending mass regularly would have displeased him.[12] "What am I to do with these *méchants* Hibernians?" Plessis exclaimed in a letter to Bishop Lartigue, without apparently expecting any helpful reply.[13]

Other influences may also have been at work on Plessis' thinking. Hugh Fenning O.P. points out that in the early part of the eighteenth century, the training of Irish friars had often been of poor quality and that for some years they had been too numerous as well. Consequently, many of them had travelled abroad in search of a position and not often with envious results. The situation had become so bad that in 1750 Propaganda issued fourteen decrees on the subject. The fourteenth decree forbade religious superiors to give the religious habit to anyone in Ireland; those wishing to join a religious order were to receive the habit only in convents in Catholic countries in which novitiates had been erected in accordance with the Constitutions of Rome. The decree ended with this sentence, "Nor may such

---

[11] AAQ RL X no. 442, Plessis to Morisset (Quebec, 25 Oct. 1821).

[12] Terrence Murphy writes, "Recent studies strongly suggest that it is a mistake to assume that immigrants direct from Ireland were in the habit of regular church attendance" ("The Emergence of Maritime Catholicism, 1781-1830" ["The Emergence of Maritime Catholicism"], *Acadiensis* 13: 2 [Spring 1984], 37).

[13] AAQ RL XI no. 220, Plessis to Lartigue (Quebec, 14 Aug. 1823).

novices return to Ireland until they have finished their course of studies, and particularly until they have a thorough grasp of dogmatic and moral theology." As a result of this, novitiates were closed for a long time, and the supply of priests dropped very low. Although the direct result was that by 1812 there were only about 250 non-diocesan clergy in the whole country of Ireland, the earlier notoriety of the Irish clergy, especially the Irish travelling friars, persisted well into the next century.[14] Terrence Murphy also recounts that a number of examples of misbehaviour on the part of Irish-born clergy occurred in Maritime Canada both before and after 1800, "involving in some cases the abuse of alcohol, in others sexual impropriety, and in still others financial chicanery and insubordination. . . . The general consensus, even at the time, was that Irish clergymen were the most frequent offenders, but individual problems arose in connection with Scottish, French, and even Canadian priests."[15] Thus, when Fr Charles Ffrench arrived in America, more than sixty years had passed since Rome's edict shutting down novitiates, but the legacy of those measures had not significantly diminished in the New World, and Ffrench was to suffer from it.

Plessis' correspondence is replete with expressions suggesting that more and more he came to equate Ffrench with this preconceived notion of undesirable Irish friars. Nor did he seem to mind how many persons he mentioned it to. Ffrench himself was shocked when Gagnon told him that Plessis had

---

[14] Hugh Fenning O.P., *The Undoing of the Friars of Ireland: A Study of the Novitiate Question in the Eighteenth Century* (Louvain: Bibliothèque de l'Université, 1972), 204-208, 339.

[15] Murphy, "The Emergence of Maritime Catholicism," 36-38. In the same essay, Murphy comments on the decline in the number of clergy in Ireland. He observes, "Indeed, recent research indicates that the number of Irish priests in relation to the Irish population had begun to decline even before the closing of the continental colleges" (34-35n.18).

Ch. 8. The Role of Nationalism in the Case 139

alluded to him, Ffrench, as a "vagabond monk."[16] To Fr Pierre Mignault, the *curé* at Halifax, Plessis confided, of Ffrench's journey to Newfoundland, "In the meantime, the souls confided to his care remain abandoned, and *that* is what one must expect from an Irish friar."[17] To Fr Morisset he commented, "Be assured that the Bishops of Ireland are too prudent to let their good subjects get away and that all these wanderers of foreign lands are merely discredited persons or those under suspicion, whom [the authorities] do not know what to do with in their own dioceses or in their monasteries." He further suggested that Morisset write to MacEachern, newly raised to the rank of bishop, to guard against "adventurer priests" who would ask him for powers to exercise in his territory.[18] And again, a year later, to the same missionary, "I am becoming more and more difficult on the admission of vagabond ecclesiastics who come from Ireland, especially monks."[19] As for Morisset himself, Plessis expressed full confidence in him, describing him to Bishop Connolly as "good and virtuous," and comparing him favorably to the "vagabond monk," Fr Charles Ffrench.[20] After Fr Ffrench had returned to Saint John in an attempt to clear his name, Plessis warned Fr Morisset that Ffrench was "prowling around" New Brunswick.[21] But it was not just Fr Ffrench, the individual,

---

[16] AAQ RL VIII no. 394, Plessis to Gagnon (Quebec, 2 Jan. 1815); AAQ NB V no. 38, Gagnon to Plessis (Bouctouche, 11 Feb. 1816).
[17] AAQ RL VIII no. 394, Plessis to Mignault (Quebec, 2 Jan. 1815).
[18] AAQ RL X no. 220, Plessis to Morisset (Quebec, 25 Oct. 1821).
[19] AAQ RL XI no. 105, Plessis to Morisset (Quebec, 27 Dec. 1822).
[20] AAQ RL X no. 506, Plessis to Connolly (Quebec, 23 Feb. 1822). Despite this statement, Plessis' admiration for Fr Morisset seems not to have been whole-hearted. He would confide to Bishop MacEachern that Morisset, whose attitude to his mission at Saint John seemed to change with each letter he wrote, was "une tête inconsistante" (ADC, 15 Aug. 1823).
[21] AAQ RL X no. 607, Plessis to Morisset (Quebec, 4 Sept. 1822). Plessis uses a form of the verb *rôder*, commonly used to describe the activities of predatory animals, as also in AAQ RL XI no. 188, Plessis to MacEachern (Quebec, 19 May 1823).

against whom his animosity was directed. "These adventurer-monks," he remarked to MacEachern, "would be much better in their convents than everywhere else."[22] In short, written expressions of Plessis' aversion to the Irish clergy, especially the friars, abound in his correspondence of the period, and his antipathy towards them in no way diminished with closer and more frequent contact.

The esteem in which Irish immigrants to the New World held good pulpit oratory is, as we have seen, another motif that recurs in the ongoing struggle between the church wardens and their prelates, both in New Brunswick and in the United States. And, in the success of this activity, a knowledge of the language of the congregation is critical. When Ffrench was leaving the Miramichi for the United States, Plessis wrote to tell him that Fr Morisset had been appointed to replace him at Bartibog. Though Morisset did not know English very well the bishop was optimistic. "He will finish learning it in a few months," he wrote to Ffrench.[23] Morisset, who was unhappy in Saint John, where he was sent three years later, knew his proficiency in English was low, but, despite Plessis' optimism, it did not improve much during his stay at either place. Still, he said, of Saint John, "Up to now, the only thing they reproach me with is of being French." This situation the congregation apparently intended to remedy by writing to Ireland "to send them a priest of their own nationality."[24] Regardless of whom they enticed to the colony, however, the archbishop had his own agenda. Of a certain Fr Walsh, even though ordained in Rome, he was immediately suspicious. "As for me," he informed Fr Patrick McMahon, who had expressed himself positively about Walsh's suitability, "He is an Irishman, a monk, already made a priest before coming to this country. The good that you say of him does not reassure me about a man who would likely have been kept in his monastery, or in his diocese, if he had really had some merit. Do not be

---

[22] AAQ RL XI no. 188, Plessis to MacEachern (19 May 1823).
[23] AAQ RL IX no. 41, Plessis to Ffrench (Quebec, 5 Nov. 1816).
[24] AAQ NB II no. 30, Morisset to Plessis (Bartibog, Sept. 1821).

surprised that I am a little distrustful, after the small amount of edification that my diocese received about messieurs Ffrench, Swiney, Carroll and McQuad."[25] The letter containing that appreciation was written just four months before Plessis' death, although, so far as Fr Ffrench was concerned, it had been an *idée fixe* for a decade. To Bishop Connolly, he had long since commented, "As for me, I am resolved never to employ any of these wandering religious who are suitable only for bringing trouble to the churches."[26]

As we know, Ffrench's affiliations with the Protestants aroused Plessis' antipathy as well. Ffrench had been a Protestant, had been brought up among them, and was quite at ease with them. Plessis, however, naturally feared contagion, and resisted it. The Saint John congregation's persistence in wanting to have a voice in the choice of its pastor, which was a Protestant custom, is once again a case in point, as is Ffrench's acceptance of Protestant contributions.[27] In general, however, any risk of contagion seems to have been all the other way as far as Fr Ffrench was concerned, for he was an extremely successful proselytiser and succeeded in converting many Protestants at every stage of his career.

Plessis' aversion to Ffrench, especially as an Irishman, seems to owe its origin, therefore, to several factors: first to the

---

[25] AAQ NB II no. 76, McMahon to Plessis (Saint John, 14 July 1825); AAQ RL XII no. 277, Plessis to McMahon (Quebec, 2 Aug. 1825). In the case of Walsh, the archbishop's apprehensions appear to have been fully justified, for, in his very next letter to Plessis, McMahon retracted his recommendation (AAQ NB II no. 77 [Saint John, 4 Oct. 1825]).

[26] AAQ RL X no. 506, Plessis to Connolly (Quebec, 23 Feb. 1822).

[27] In these matters, Plessis was fighting against the current of custom in the Maritimes. Terrence Murphy writes that the practice of Protestants helping Catholics to build their churches was a common one in the cities, and that the Protestants often attended Catholic sermons ("The Emergence of Maritime Catholicism," 44). As his correspondence shows, Ffrench had no compunction about furthering this sort of participation.

natural apprehension of a conquered nation towards its conqueror, and, by association, towards those who spoke the conqueror's language; secondly, to certain widespread notions of the Irish as a group and of Irish friars in particular; thirdly, to the fact that the Saint John congregation found Ffrench much more to their liking than they did Plessis' own choices for them, their persistence in this idea being at odds with Plessis' concept of what was due his own authority; fourthly, to a handful of unhappy experiences Plessis had with other Irish clergy; and finally, to Ffrench's own behaviour. That Ffrench's ideas of church discipline were not fully in line with Plessis' own is not surprising, but it is to be noted that in all major matters, once Plessis gave him a direct order to act or to cease acting in a certain way, Ffrench immediately obeyed. That Plessis was, and remained, only too willing to accept Morisset's account of rumours circulating about Ffrench might be attributed, therefore, to all these factors working together on the mind of an overworked and exasperated prelate.

Luca Codignola writes that ethnic rivalry during the early nineteenth century manifested even more virulence in the United States than in Canada.[28] This was partly because, side by side with the trustee controversies, there flourished within the American church deep and durable racial prejudices. Among the Catholics, the French, the German, and the Irish were the most discernible national groups striving to establish or maintain dominance. Appeals from all three communities flowed into Rome for the vindication of claims and the righting of perceived wrongs. The most irritating of these latter for the Irish was the poor representation of their clergy in the ranks of the United States hierarchy. In 1817 five of the six episcopal seats in North America were filled by men of Gallic ancestry, this at a time when the French constituted a fast-diminishing minority of

---

[28] Codignola, "Conflict or Consensus," 57.

Catholics in every North American see except that of Quebec.[29] Given the democratic and republican ideals espoused and championed by most of the Irish flooding into the country, as well as by the basic tenets of the United States itself, it was inevitable that a redress of the imbalance in the prelacy would be widely advocated at the grass roots level.

There was also a widespread conviction that there existed a basic incompatibility in temperament between French bishops and Irish priests; this idea was articulated to Propaganda in September of 1820 by the Augustinian missionary, Fr. Robert Browne O.S.A.[30] Furthermore, it was commonly held by the rank and file Irish that the French bishops had a low opinion of the Irish clergy, and generally preferred not to employ them. Certainly, Archbishop Plessis' correspondence indicates that this was true of him, at least insofar as those clergy who left Ireland were concerned, and remarks made by Archbishop Ambrose Maréchal of Baltimore, especially in his report to Rome on 16 October 1818, strongly support the notion that Plessis' bias found its echo among other French prelates.[31] Under these

---

[29] In 1817, the episcopal seats of the continent were fixed at Quebec (Plessis), Boston (Cheverus), New York (Connolly), Baltimore (Maréchal), Bardstown (Flaget), and Louisiana (Dubourg).

[30] Browne's report, which was on the state of Catholicism in Washington, D.C., Virginia, the Carolinas, Georgia, and Louisiana, was published by Kevin F. Dwyer O.S.A. in *Records of the American Catholic Historical Society of Philadelphia* 103: 1 (Spring 1992), 41-61.

[31] Among other charges, Maréchal wrote to Propaganda that it was neither the Americans nor the English nor the newcomers from other European nations who had disturbed or were causing turmoil at Charleston, Norfolk, Philadelphia etc. but Irish priests, addicted to drunkenness or ambition, allied with those whom they recruited by many and various deceits (*Catholic Historical Review* 1 [1915-1916], 445-446). According to Ronin Murther, "The friction between the Irish and French in the U.S. grew in intensity with the cause of Irish freedom [in Ireland]. . . . The first period of [Archbishop Maréchal's] administration (1817-1821) was marked by his attempt to convince

conditions, and because the French-speaking bishops lacked sufficient English-speaking clergy to minister to their English-speaking parishioners in any case, they were reduced to appointing to cures priests whose English language skills were rudimentary if extant at all.[32] Such practices were depressing impedimenta to the progress of the church, especially among a group where a high premium was placed on accomplished preaching. Furthermore, it appears that there was no attempt to recruit, in any well directed fashion, young, qualified and proven men from the ranks of the Irish clergy.

The controversy in New York is an excellent illustration of the intertwining of trusteeism and national or ethnic bias, and not just because the conflict broke out there first, was unarguably far more intense than elsewhere, and, with one or two interruptions, lasted longer.[33]

In his report of the visit he made to New York at the request of Cardinal Fontana in 1820, the recently minted Archbishop of

---

Rome that there was no discrimination against the Irish by the French prelates, to make Propaganda aware of the rebellious attitude of some of the Irish-born priests" ("Ambrose Maréchal," 211-212). Christopher Kauffman writes that Maréchal's anti-Irish prejudice grew stronger as the years passed (*Tradition and Transformation in Catholic Culture: The Priests of Saint Sulpice in the United States from 1791 to the Present* [New York: Macmillan, 1988], 103).

[32] For example, Fr Joseph Morisset, Ffrench's replacement at Bartibog in 1816 (AAQ RL IX no. 41, Plessis to Ffrench [Quebec, 5 Nov. 1816]). See also Peter Guilday, *The Catholic Church in Virginia (1815-1822)* (New York: United States Catholic Historical Society, 1924), xxvii.

[33] The origins of the first contest date back to 1786 when Fr Andrew Nugent lost the favour of the Board of Trustees, was suspended by Archbishop Carroll and led a rump of diehard parishioners into schism. The trustees were compelled to sue for the return of church property, which Nugent had withheld. According to Gerald Fogarty, the parishioners supported Nugent because he was "a better preacher" ("Lay Trusteeism," 656).

Quebec expressed to Propaganda his innermost feelings about the Irish, as well as about Fr Ffrench, Bishop Connolly, and the state of the New York church generally. There, in a passage already cited, he referred to Connolly's followers as "the Irish rabble that Fr Ffrench knows how to incite and attach to himself, an ignorant and wild populace always ready to take sides, without thinking." Expressions of his ethnic preferences with respect to the episcopacy of the United States are also to be found in the same document, for in it he confessed himself "obliged to repeat" that, in the United States the French bishops were much loved and respected by their diocesans, and that any complaints against them were initiated by "Irish monks, ambitious vagabonds, who to the misfortune of these dioceses, would like to occupy the highest positions there." He further recommended that caution be exercised in dealing with petitions that had large subscriber lists appended.[34] The inference to be deduced from this latter recommendation is that the Irish signers either did not know or did not care what they were signing, or else that some of the signatures were false.

Bishop Plessis' bias was shared by other French speakers in the parish of Old Saint Peter's, not the least of whom was Fr Pierre Malou. As one of Bishop Connolly's strongest and most active supporters during the most critical phase of the conflict, Fr Ffrench, as we have noted, endured abusive and slanderous attacks from the trustee party and its associates. So, for instance, Malou, the clerical advisor of the rebellious coterie, was the first to charge the Dominican with anti-French sentiments. Malou was not, of course, French, but rather a francophone Belgian. When Ffrench addressed Plessis in mid-January of 1822 he revealed his awareness of the misrepresentations and falsehoods that were being spread abroad about him. He had been, he told Plessis, depicted as an "'enemy of the French nation,' also of speaking 'in a very disrespectful manner of the Venerable

---

[34] APF LDNA vol. 2 (1792-1830) pt. 2, 475-478, Plessis to Fontana (Quebec, 6 Sept. 1820).

French Prelates and Priests of the United States.'" The friar emphatically denied those charges, and solemnly rejected all such accusations as untrue. As we know, Bishop Plessis did not reply directly to this letter, and in the one he sent to Connolly refusing the faculties Ffrench had asked for, made no mention of the Dominican's disavowal.[35]

One might cite, as a representative of some of the anti-Irish laity, a Monsieur Jean Sorbieu, who was a prominent member of the French Catholic community. Writing to Pierre Toussaint, a friend who had gone to live in France, Sorbieu inquired, "Who are these *malheureux sauvages irlandais* who think they are giving a great proof of their Catholicism?" And, in a further letter to the same recipient, "I assign the little respect which these *malheureux Irlandais* have for religion to their ignorance, the majority of whom are Catholics in name only."[36]

The charge of francophobism was one of those examined by the Consultor to Propaganda, with embarrassing consequences for the appellants. Mazzetti posed these questions, "What meaning shall we attach to the fact that, as soon as Ffrench said some mean things about French Bishops, and began to compete with Father Malou, they began to attack him? What meaning shall we attach to the fact that Monseigneur Maréchal, the Archbishop, attaches more importance to the events of New York than to those of Norfolk or Charleston?"[37] His implication here is that Maréchal had taken sides because of national bias and that Malou had reacted too strongly to negative remarks

---

[35] AAQ EU IV no. 35, Ffrench to Plessis (New York, 18 Jan. 1822); AAQ RL X no. 506, Plessis to Connolly (Quebec, 23 Feb. 1822). In his first long letter of complaint against Ffrench, Malou had told Archbishop Plessis that Ffrench had spoken out against French priests and bishops (AAQ EU IV no. 18 [New York, 9 Dec. 1818]).

[36] Sorbieu to Toussaint, no. 40 (Rouen, 1 June 1820); same to same, no. 47 (n.p., n.d.). In Leo R. Ryan, "Pierre Toussaint 'God's Image Carved in Ebony,'" *Historical Records and Studies* 25 (1 June 1935), 39-58.

[37] Voto, 9.

from Ffrench. It would be unrealistic to assume that there was no ethnic bias at all on Ffrench's side, or that Ffrench had never once made a comment that might be interpreted as anti-French. We simply do not know, and so Mazzetti's comments imply neither Ffrench's innocence of such remarks nor his guilt. However, no expressions of any such sentiments have been discovered in Ffrench's correspondence.[38]

The existence of Propaganda's decree that, along with Malou and Taylor, Ffrench should leave New York, has been the one fact held onto by his detractors since that time. The fact that seems to have been forgotten is that Propaganda did not pronounce Ffrench guilty of anything, and that Mazzetti's judgment was harsher on Fr Malou, and even on Archbishops Plessis and Maréchal, than it was on Ffrench. In effect, it upheld Bishop Connolly's position, and his protection of Ffrench. That Fr Ffrench was the object of so many negative remarks in so many documents of the period must be attributed at least in part to manifestations of political or ethnic bias on the part of his detractors. These included, of course, not only those living in New York and actively engaged in the controversy, but also those who played a role in encouraging and perpetuating the animosity of others. Unfortunately for Fr Charles Ffrench, numbered among these were some powerful figures, foremost among whom was the Reverend Joseph-Octave Plessis, Archbishop of Quebec.

In defence of Archbishop Plessis, it must be noted that at least some of his apparent bias against the idea of appointing Irish prelates to North American dioceses was actually against the notion of placing non-American priests in positions of authority. Laval Laurent observes that Plessis "never approved of the appointment of a foreigner to an American episcopal see

---

[38] In his outline of American church politics, Gerald P. Fogarty writes that the two sides in the New York trustee dispute illustrated the basic Irish-French tension of the American Church, and that Ffrench was unjustly accused of francophobism ("Lay Trusteeism," 656-659).

and he never supported the nomination of a misfit candidate, even if he were a Frenchman. According to him, before governing a diocese, a candidate must first make a stay in the country."[39] Archbishop Plessis' position with respect to the American episcopate may well have been founded on this rational basis, which was shared, to some extent at least, by Archbishop Maréchal. However, his attitude towards Irish clergy in general was by no means so tolerant, and there is no doubt that as early as 1817 he had chosen never to speak well of one friar in particular, namely Charles Dominic Ffrench O.P.

It is impossible, at this remove in time, to unravel all the threads of nationalistic, religious, political,[40] and personal motivations that may have played a role in events in New York during the period 1818-1826, or even in those of New Brunswick during Fr Ffrench's sojourns there. That nationalistic sentiments were a negative influence on his career is nevertheless certain. That he himself was biased in favour of the Irish is, of course, possible as well, perhaps even likely, despite his reticence to commit that prejudice to paper. Patrick Dignan comments, "Only men of the very loftiest vision escaped the shackles of nationalistic feeling at that period of American Catholic

---

[39] Laurent, *Québec et l'Eglise*, 199.

[40] Patrick Carey suggests that the trustee struggle in New York may have had a specific political dimension. He writes: "The political allegiances of Catholics in New York are difficult to determine, but it appears that many of the older and original trustees of St. Peter's from 1787 to 1819 were Federalists; they suffered defeat during the trustee elections of 1819 and 1820 in part because of the rising tide of Irish democrats. Evidence for this can be seen in the incumbent trustees' opposition to Francis Cooper, a leading Catholic democratic politician in the city and an Episcopal supporter" (*People, Priests, and Prelates: Ecclesiastical Democracy and the Tensions of Trusteeism* [Notre Dame: University of Notre Dame Press, 1987], 137). Certainly Malou's correspondence reveals that among the clergy he, for one, was in vehement opposition to Mr Cooper's having any authority at St. Peter's.

history."[41] Unfortunately for Fr Ffrench, if any such men were active either in Canada or in the northeastern United States during the period when he was a missionary there, they do not appear to have played an influential role in his career.

---

[41] "Peter Anthony Malou," 94. Comparing the modern era with that of the early Catholic church in the United States, Fogarty writes, "No longer do American bishops espouse the ethnocentrism that tainted even great men like Archbishop Maréchal and Bishop Connolly" ("Lay Trusteeism," 658).

View of Partridge Island and the Harbour of St. John, 1835, by Mary G. Hall. Courtesy New Brunswick Museum, Saint John, N.B. (W1545).

Chapter 9

FR FFRENCH'S CASE
AND THE PASSAGE OF TIME

History is constantly being rewritten, and historians are continually obliged to change their interpretations of past events, perhaps even to amend their records of those events themselves. New facts come to light. New attitudes reveal old ones to be mistaken, biased or influenced by peripheral factors. But "facts" not investigated–for it is not possible to research every fact for every project, hence some data must be accepted on faith–do not get changed in history books and may simply be repeated in written commentary until, possibly even by chance, the truth comes to light. The role of King Richard III in the assassination of the princes in the tower is a celebrated case in point. The history of Fr Ffrench's reputation belongs to this same category, albeit on a lesser scale, and so blame is rarely to be attached to any historian who has delineated his case inaccurately. Actually, it is to the words of some of the participants of the dramas in which Ffrench was involved that just cause might be attributed. And, in attributing cause, one must keep in mind that some kinds of rumours and anecdotes, whether true or not, tend to linger among a populace long years after the actors in a piece have disappeared.

A few specific examples of this phenomenon as it applies to Fr Ffrench might be useful.

Placide Gaudet, a well-known and reputable writer of the Acadian community writing some hundred years ago, is the earliest figure of the past century to have retailed some of the tales about Fr Ffrench. In a letter of 1903 to Mgr Henri Têtu, he asserted: (1) that Fr Ffrench had been found at Madawaska by

Bishop Plessis and transferred from there to the Miramichi; (2) that he was not sure whether the Dominican's residence had been at Bartibog or at Burnt Church, although he correctly identified Fr François-Mathias Huot as Ffrench's immediate predecessor in the mission and stated that Ffrench had been the first English-speaking missionary in the district; (3) that Ffrench had served the Neguac station from November 1813 to August 1816, but that he had left a very bad reputation at Neguac and everywhere else he went in the missions of New Brunswick; (4) that the old men of Neguac had told him Ffrench had been interdicted; and (5) that another old man had informed him Ffrench had had a bastard child with an Acadian girl. Gaudet asserted that, while looking over some notes he had taken many years before, he had recently found the name of the girl the Dominican had debauched.[1]

One can quickly detect the distortions in Gaudet's account. First, Ffrench had not been transferred from Madawaska to the Miramichi but had spent a year in Quebec City before he was sent to the latter. Secondly, the statement that Gaudet did not know whether Ffrench had resided at Bartibog or at Burnt Church indicates that his sources of information lacked certainty. Thirdly, Ffrench's reputation was *not* tarnished everywhere he went, for documents show that he had many supporters, both in Saint John and elsewhere in New Brunswick. Fourthly, Ffrench had neither been suspended nor interdicted; in fact, he had already requested and received an exeat. To be precise, his faculties had then been revoked, and a suspension eventually drawn up and entrusted to Fr McMahon, but it was to be published only if McMahon deemed it necessary, which he did not. Finally, there was no proof whatsoever that Fr Ffrench had sired a child in New Brunswick and much evidence against. Despite these differences between rumour and fact, it is not difficult to understand how such a distorted view could be accepted as true, for, among other things, Ffrench's *A Short*

---

[1] AAQ NE V no. 166, Gaudet to Têtu (Quebec, 23 Sept. 1903).

Memoir was not likely available to Gaudet, nor, for that matter, Mary Toole's letter of recantation to Archbishop Plessis.

A little more than a decade after Gaudet conveyed these ideas to Têtu, Frederick Zwierlein contributed to a festschrift an article on the American episcopal nominations of the early nineteenth century. In his essay, Zwierlein devoted some space to the trustee quarrel in New York. Interestingly enough, he employed much of the argumentation and language of the anti-episcopal party. Thus he depicted Bishop Connolly essentially as, "according to all, a man of virtue, but . . . 'weak and indecisive,'" adding that Connolly's administration "was disastrous for religion."[2] Clearly, Zwierlein, like Malou and Plessis, did not really know his man very well; otherwise, he would have taken into account the fearlessness and determination that Bishop Connolly, then mere Fr Connolly, had displayed in the face of Napoleon's intimidation. During the latter's occupation of Rome, his imprisonment of Pope Pius VI, and the sequestration of church property in 1798, Fr Connolly had kept a lonely vigil over the interests of San Clemente so long as the French remained in the city. Even more, he had displayed his singular strength of character and courage by refusing to take an oath of allegiance to Bonaparte, not once but three times.[3] These actions could never have been interpreted as those of a

---

[2] Frederick Zwierlein, "Les nominations épiscopales aux premiers temps de l'épiscopat américain," in *Mélanges d'Histoire offerts à Charles Moeller*, 2 vols. (Louvain: Université de Louvain, 1914), vol. 2, 533. Zwierlein gives Malou's letters of 9 Dec. 1818 and 15 Jan. 1819 to Bishop Plessis as his sources for these particular statements.

[3] Leonard E. Boyle, San Clemente Miscellany I The Community of SS Sisto e Clemente in Roma (Rome: S. Clemente, 1977). One recent account of Connolly's life relates this particular war-time incident and stresses quite heavily his qualities of courage, determination and decisiveness. See Anna M. Donnelly, "Connolly, John (1747/48 or 1751-1825)," in *Encyclopedia of American Catholic History*, eds. Michael Glazier and Thomas J. Shelley (Collegeville, Minn.: Liturgical Press, 1997), 373-374.

weak and irresolute man. Thus, in refusing to accept statements that Connolly was not firm enough, Fr Mazzetti, the Consultor to Propaganda, who assessed the New York quarrel and concluded that Connolly had been capably assertive in events there, would have known very well what proof of the prelate's decisiveness had already been shown. In making his argument, however, Zwierlein relied heavily on letters written by Fr Malou and probably knew nothing of Connolly's Napoleonic adventure.

Another twenty years later, Rev. Ivanhoë Caron presented before the Royal Society of Canada a paper in which several of the old charges made against Bishop Connolly, as well as against Frs Carbry and Ffrench, were resurrected and a few new ones introduced. In it Caron asserted (1) that Ffrench had taken refuge in the Diocese of New York after having been chased out of New Brunswick; (2) that the Dominican had not delayed quarrelling with Fr Malou; (3) that he had caused Malou to be suspect in the eyes of Bishop Connolly; (4) that Bishop Panet, as he was then, had refused to give Willcocks the documents (which Caron seems implicitly to have assumed existed) wherein Ffrench's misconduct in New Brunswick was openly detailed (*nemo dat quod non habet*); (5) that the new bishop, John Connolly, did not have the necessary strength to master the troubles in the diocese; (6) that Monseigneur Plessis' intervention had been called for, since (Caron stated) Bishop Connolly had kept silent in the trustee dispute; and, finally, (7) that Ffrench had found refuge in Philadelphia when he was ordered to leave New York, and went from there to Saint John.[4]

We now know that not only had Ffrench not been chased out of New Brunswick when he went to New York, he had already received a proper exeat; that Malou himself had been precipitous in his quarrel with Ffrench and openly in rebellion against his bishop; that Panet had been in no position to furnish

---

[4] Ivanhoë Caron, "Mgr Joseph-Octave Plessis, Archevêque de Québec, et les Premiers Evêques Catholiques des Etats-Unis," *Mémoires de la Société Royale du Canada*, 3rd series, 28 (1934), 126-131.

Willcocks with details of Ffrench's "misconduct" other than, possibly, Mary Toole's original letters denouncing Ffrench and summaries of the reports of rumours from other missionaries; that Connolly was not weak and had actively attempted to quell the rebels; that Plessis had been requested to intervene by Malou but not by Propaganda; and that, although Ffrench had been offered a post in Philadelphia, he had turned it down in favour of a visit to Saint John. Caron named as his sources for the "facts" mentioned above a number of letters, including, however, only one each from Fr Ffrench and Bishop Connolly, but five from Malou, one from Willcocks, one from Archbishop Maréchal, and four from Archbishop Plessis, among these last his report to Cardinal Fontana, wrongly identified as being of 7 Sept. 1820 instead of 6 Sept. In other words Caron chose to rely on or had recourse only to those sources that the possession of a more complete picture of the situation now reveals as insufficient.

The subject was treated anew in 1945 by Laval Laurent in his book on Quebec and the American church. Two chapters, "Mgr Plessis et les 'trustees' américains (1815-1825)" and "Monseigneur Plessis et la nomination des évêques américains (1820-1825)," contain the pertinent sections of his argument. According to Laurent, Ffrench had arrived in North America intent on establishing a house of his Order, an assertion for which Laurent provided no supporting data, and indeed for which there is none. He claimed also that the Dominican had not been pleased with his appointment to the Miramichi mission and had frequently absented himself "on the pretext" of collecting for charity. In fact, the Miramichi mission may or may not have pleased Fr Ffrench, but there is no real evidence one way or the other on this matter in his correspondence. On the correlative charge, so far as is provable Ffrench was only twice away from his mission, namely, when he journeyed to Halifax to solicit funds for the construction of the Saint John church, and when he visited Newfoundland for the same purpose. Laurent further claimed that Ffrench had inspired Malou's recall by Fr Anthony Kohlmann, the Superior of the Jesuits. While it is true that

Bishop Connolly requested that favour of Fr Kohlmann, there is no evidence that Ffrench played any role in the transaction. As to Laurent's assertion that "the intruder [Ffrench] left the place [Saint John] only after the arrival of abbé Patrick McMahon, successor to abbé Carroll; on this occasion the parishioners chased him out," the latter comment in no way conforms to reality. Finally, Laurent assumed that Ffrench was secularized, if not when he first arrived in New York then at least later on; no written source is offered for this statement, which is, of course, incorrect.[5]

Another significant factor that has helped to perpetuate inaccuracies has been the frequent necessity for researchers to rely, for information tangential to their principal investigations, on the published reports of archbishopric correspondence in publications such as *L'Archiviste de la Province de Québec*. Extremely valuable as such reports are, their use is not without its perils. Many of Archbishop Plessis' letters are inventoried, for example, in the 1927-1928 and 1928-1929 volumes, and references to Fr Charles Ffrench are numerous in them. Unfortunately, however, all the "facts" reported in those letters, and consequently in the *Archiviste* reports, are what the archbishop believed to be the truth, but they are not necessarily the truth itself. Secondly, the more frequently that perceived facts are communicated to others, the greater is the possibility of further error in their dissemination, and so the error in Ffrench's case has occasionally been amplified. One finds, for example, in the *Archiviste* report of Plessis' letter of 15 Aug. 1815 to Ffrench himself, a reference to the archbishop's reproach to the Dominican of not having written to him during the two years the latter had been on the Miramichi; in this case, however, a probable mis-reading of "dix ans" for "deux ans" in the original has resulted in the *Archiviste* indicating that Ffrench had been on his mission for *ten* years instead of two.[6] This is a very small

---

[5] Laurent, *Québec et L'Eglise*, 159-160, 165, 174.

[6] *Rapport de l'Archiviste de la Province de Québec pour 1927-1928* (Quebec, Rédempti Paradis, 1928), 309.

error indeed, but it is one that, coupled with a large accumulation of other negative remarks about him, has done Fr Ffrench's reputation no service.

It can be readily seen how one or two slight discrepancies in a story can lead eventually to a complete skewing of the facts. Though the details may have varied slightly from account to account over the years, the tendency to portray Fr Ffrench in a negative light has continued right up to the present time. Fr Ffrench, according to most accounts, was a friar guilty of sexual immorality and probably of financial fraud, convicted by a strong bishop in Quebec but protected by a weak one in New York, to the unhappiness of nearly all. Ffrench's career after his departure from New York, though without blemish of any kind, has been more or less ignored by critics.

As a result of these and other factors, the bad press Ffrench has received even in recent years appears to rely, in one degree or another, upon all the old charges, rumours and stories that have made up the accepted wisdom about the friar. Marianna O'Gallagher, for example, observed in 1983 that "the wanderings of the Dominican Father Charles French [sic] can be followed, as Bishops sent good priests after him to try to repair the scandal of his passing."[7] Writing that Ffrench had been accused of "libertine behaviour in Ireland, Portugal, New Brunswick, Quebec, and New York, and of personal use of funds collected under the pretence of building a new church," Luca Codignola referred, in 1988, to Ffrench as a priest "of dubious virtue."[8] In 1993, Terrence Murphy alleged that "evidence came to light that he [Ffrench] had been guilty of sexual impropriety" during his tenure at Bartibog and that, "in the face of mounting evidence of irregular conduct on his part, Plessis stiffened in his refusal to appoint him."[9] As we have taken pains to demonstrate,

---

[7] Marianna O'Gallagher S.C.H., "Irish Priests in the Diocese of Quebec in the Nineteenth Century," CCHA *Study Sessions* 50 (1983), 407.

[8] Codignola, "Conflict or Consensus," 58.

[9] Murphy, "Trusteeism in Atlantic Canada," 141.

this "mounting evidence," to which, in effect, all of the above remarks refer, consisted of the reports, slanders, falsehoods, and accusations which gathered about Ffrench's name and doings in New York and New Brunswick and which were all interpreted in but one fashion at Quebec. If there had been incontrovertible evidence of Ffrench's guilt, there would have been no reason for Archbishop Plessis not to report the case to Rome as he was required to do, a fact that was, of course, later pointed out in the report of the Consultor to Propaganda.

This is by no means to imply that the remarks of these critics are indications of imperfect scholarship. On the contrary, all the works in which they appear are valuable and thought-provoking studies. But every one of them has necessarily focused on a personage other than Ffrench or on an event in which Ffrench was not the principal player. In other words, there has been no reason for writers to pay close scrutiny to a matter more or less peripheral to the picture being investigated. Unfortunately, too, no published study to date has had as its subject Fr Charles Dominic Ffrench, perhaps because his cause was never of central importance to anyone but himself.[10]

---

[10] One article focused completely on Fr Ffrench does exist. This is, of course, the brief biography by Arthur M. Osborne, "Charles Ffrench, Pioneer Missionary," CCHA *Report* 19 (1952), 77-86. In it, Osborne offers nothing but praise for Ffrench, but he either passes over or is completely unaware of the rumours and accusations with which Ffrench had to deal; in addition, the article makes numerous errors of fact. The only other work exclusively on Ffrench is, to our knowledge, Fr Victor O'Daniel's "Appendix E," already referred to several times in this study. However, it was never published and its existence appears to have been largely unknown or ignored by critics until recently. Laval Laurent, for example, lists in his bibliography only O'Daniel's book, *The Dominican Province of Saint Joseph*, saying that the biographical summary it contains on Ffrench (148-157) is a little bit idealized (*Québec et L'Eglise*, 159). On the other hand, the recently published *Encyclopedia of American Catholic History* contains, in Anna M. Donnelly's biography of Bishop John Connolly (373-374), a full reference to O'Daniel's project of which the "Appendix E" forms a

There is a tremendous gap between existing reports of Fr Ffrench's personal qualities and level of service during the more than thirty years he spent in New England, and his earlier record offering pride of place to the rumours and written statements circulated about him during his eight years in Canada and New York. Was he a "bad priest," or was he the victim of a conspiracy nourished by his enemies and perpetuated by a well-meaning but badly informed bishop? Which version of his life should be believed? Certainly, not the first one, which we have attempted to demonstrate is a thesis without substantiation.

This is not to claim that Ffrench was quite the paragon of virtue depicted in the glowing obituary devoted to him by Bishop Fitzpatrick in the pages of the Boston Memoranda. That Bishop Fitzpatrick was sincere in his praise of Ffrench, without desire to exaggerate even under the weight of his own loss, there is no reason to doubt. Charitable and forgiving Ffrench may have been, as Fitzpatrick claimed. Nevertheless, sharp words may well have issued from his lips on more than one occasion when he was provoked, thereby arousing resentment or even vindictiveness in the heart of his interlocutor. He may even, as Fr Malou suggested, have imbibed too freely or frequented low company in the taverns. Fr Ffrench may have been guilty of all these things and more. But one thing is clear: the root accusations against him, the charges on which his negative reputation has rested for so many years, were baseless, shifting like quicksand in which all of Ffrench's efforts to restore his own good name in Canada and the United States were futile. Whatever the Dominican's shortcomings, he deserved better.

Nearly two hundred years have passed since Fr Charles Dominic Ffrench O.P. first set foot on the shores of North America. It is time that his character was rehabilitated.

---

part. The additional publicity generated by this recent reference should make O'Daniel's unpublished manuscript better known to scholars in future years than it has been in the past.

(1)

Appendix A[1]

A SHORT

MEMOIR,

WITH SOME DOCUMENTS IN VINDICATION OF THE
CHARGES MADE BY MALICIOUS PERSONS
AGAINST THE CHARACTER OF THE

REV. CHARLES FFRENCH

ADDRESSED

TO THE

Roman Catholics

OF BRITISH AMERICA, AND OF THE UNITED STATES

———

Printed at the City Gazette Office, near the Post-Office, Saint John, New-Brunswick.

---

[1] These pages are transcribed from the photocopy of an original document in possession of the Georgetown University Archives; it is no doubt the document Victor O'Daniel located after a long search. Photocopies can now be found in the Archives of the Archdiocese of Quebec, the Centre for Acadian Studies in Moncton, and the Archives of the Diocese of Saint John. The beginning of each new page of the original is indicated in this transcription by a number in bold-face type either at the left-hand margin or within the text.

(2)

(3)

Rev. Charles Ffrench

To his Beloved Brethren of the Roman Catholic Communion, residing in the British Provinces of the CANADAS, NOVA SCOTIA, NEW-BRUNSWICK, NEW-FOUNDLAND, *and in the* UNITED STATES OF AMERICA:

DEARLY BELOVED BRETHREN,

A SENSE of gratitude for the many favors and kindnesses which you have conferred upon me during many years residence amongst you, induces me to dedicate to you the following MEMOIR, and to submit the annexed documents. They were expressly constructed by the Congregations of this City and Miramichi, the French Inhabitants of the Settlements of Nigawick and of Bay de Wind, as a vindication of my character.–Herein you can trace the detestable schemes of malicious persons, for the purpose of injuring me in your good opinion, and of degrading me as a Clergyman and a Christian.–Wretched mortals ! could they obtain no better employment than (Judas like) to betray the interests of Religion, and to deprive a Clergyman of his peace and tranquility of mind?–The privations and hardships I indured for several years on a laborious mission in a rude and severe clime; often times engaged on journies in which I had to ascend either the steep and craggy rocks, or make my way through lonely (4) woods, where the bear and other savage wild beasts would feign dispute a passage with me; other times traversing boisterous seas to seek assistance to build Churches for Catholic worship, in places where there were none ever erected before; were pastimes in comparison with the troubles and anxieties of mind which I suffered at New-York.–They were occasioned by a few discontented persons who on being discontinued as Trustees, or deprived of the office of Church Temporalities, an office which they monopolized to themselves during a great number of years. These men were so chagrined by the measure, that they seemed as if seized by a fit of frenzy; they spoke as lunatics; they treated with most unbecoming language Bishop CONNOLLY, a pious, prudent, wise and learned prelate; they poured out invectives against the Congregation at large, respectable even in its numbers; comprising several thousands of souls–they levelled their utmost resentment against me, as being the chief agent of their humiliation. The *authority* of the *Church*, the *rights* of the *Congregation* and the *adjustment* of ACCOUNTS, were in their eyes at that time treasonable expressions.

They circulated printed letters wherein they charged me with canonical censures. His Grace the Arch Bishop of Quebec rebuked them for their *mistake*, I should call it a wiful [sic] error.–They charged me with crimes which they affirmed had taken place in this Province; they charged me with robbing the funds of our Church in this City. I justified my character at a Court of Justice at New-York, and put my accusers to the blush; my enemies were equally unsuccessful in their BEEF-STEAK PLOT; it was discovered and the falsehood detected, notwithstanding the advantages which were taken of the absence of Mr. GREGORY DILLON, a gentleman of truth and honor–he was the only witness of the transaction so grossly misrepresented, and if he were present at the time the falsehood was spread, he would instantly confront the vile calumniators.

(5) From communications which I had received at New-York of plots carrying on in this Province by hired agents, I was desirous to come hither in order to find them out and bring matters to an elucidation. Circumstances so turned out that it became necessary for me the beginning of last spring to set out for St. John. I received advices from Messrs. CROOKSHANKS & JOHNSTON my correspondents, to hasten on, for my property was just going to be sold and would be sacrificed.

The ship Spectator first offered for this place; I took my passage in her, and with tears of affection parted with sincere friends; friends from whom I had always received every sympathy in my afflictions, every assistance in my wants,* and sailed the 12th April, promising ourselves a short and prosperous voyage, but had not proceeded two days when the vessel sprung a leak, and shortly after filled with water; we all took to the long boat 27 in number, and after contending twelve hours with a heavy sea and surrounded by a thick fog, we got safe ashore near New-Port, Rhode-Island. I lost my fine Library, together with many valuable effects, and papers of consequence to me; also the testimonials of my esteemed friend the Bishop of New-York, and the excellent letters of the Trustees of St. Peter's Church. Under these disadvantages yet I was kindly received and very hospitably treated by the amiable Bishop of Boston, (6) whose kindness I shall ever with gratitude recollect, also by the Rev. Gentlemen of his establishment among whom the Rev. Mr. Taylor treated me with great civility, *It is with much pleasure I mention, we have forgotten all past controversies, and are become mutual and cordial friends.* I shall likewise never forget the kindness of Messrs. M'Namarra, Day, Flahavan, Finnigan, Dowling, and others.–With no small regret I left Boston, and the amiable Bishop and his Clergymen saw me on board the vessel in which I embarked for St. John via East-port. On my arrival I have been welcomed by the inhabitants of every denomination; our Brethren in this City who differ with us in religious opinion, are a kind, unprejudiced and hospitable people refined in their manners; they have been very partial to me, and have contributed very liberally towards the building of our church–The relation of my persecutions at New-York excited in the minds of the Congregation a lively indignation; they regretted I had not long before made a communication of them for they said they could not rely on the vague reports that occasionally came from New-York and other parts of the United States. They proposed

---

* My leading friends to whom I owe everlasting obligations are Majors Noon and Mulden, Charles Mahon, Esq. A. D. Duff, Esq. Portuguese Consul; Edward P. Gallagher, Esq. James Joseph M'Donnell, Esq. Captain Lawrence Power, Frederick Barber, Esq. Messrs. Thomas Wymbs & M'Nulty, Dominick Lynch, Esq. & Co. Dr. Sweeny, Mr. Hugh O'Hair, Banker; Mr. Michael O'Connor, Michael H. Buoyer, Esq. and friends in the Bowery; Mr. Devoy and friends in the Swamp; Robt. Dillon, Esq. Gregory Dillon, Esq. Mr. Francis M'Murray, Mr. George Bowen, Mr. Michael Daly, Mr. Patrick Phelan, James Matthews, Esq. Peter Harmony, Esq. Dennis M'Carthy, Esq. Mr. Thomas Kinsly, Brooklyn; Mr. Garret Byrn, Mr. Andrew Dooly, Messrs. Terrence & John Quin, Messrs. Daniel & C. Cashman, Mr. Thomas Mooney.

many modes for redress which I could not attend to, being obliged to leave them for the moment and proceed to Norton, King's County, to look to my property. I found it in the hands of the Sheriff. A Mr. Secord and others made oath that I left this Country with the intention of defrauding them of considerable sums of money, which I owed them, hereupon the Judge of the Supreme Court of Fredericton issued an order to sell the property for the benefit of the Creditors, agreeably to an act of the Legislature of this Province made in default of absconding debtors,–I arrived just in time to prevent the Sale. Thus Secord's views were quite frustrated; he thought to have had the property at a very low price; his claim for so many hundreds of pounds sterling, proved not only ideal, but on ballancing our accounts the decision of the Court was in my favour 5s. 10d.–One story is good (7) the old proverb says, until the other is told; this saying was verified in the case before us. While I was thus employed in making strait the ways, the congregation here occasionally met, and arranged matters much to my satisfaction.–On my return three Gentlemen waited on me and presented me with a letter containing enclosed papers, of which the following are copies.

St. John, June 10th, 1822.

REV. SIR,

We the undersigned are a Committee appointed by a Meeting of the Roman Catholic congregation of this City to present your Reverence with the enclosed document, signed by the members of the Catholic body. We beg leave at the same time to express our alacrity in complying with these injunctions, and more particularly as the document we have the honor to hand you, we trust will support the cause of injured innocence, while at the same time that it unmasks the villainy of the sacreligious wretch who had the audacity to impeach it.

(Signed)   THOMAS WATERS,
                                                PATRICK MURPHY,
                                                PHILIP KEHOE.

To the Rev. Charles Ffrench.

An adjourned meeting of the Roman Catholic congregation of this City was convened at the house of Mr. Patrick Murphy, Church-street on the 6th inst.

Mr. William Cummins was called to the Chair, and Mr. Philip Kehoe, appointed Secretary.

The Chairman addressed the meeting in an handsome manner and at some length; he bestowed much praise on the talents, the good and edifying conduct of the Rev. Mr. FFRENCH, during the time of his abode in this City, and concluded by adverting to the object that now called them together, which is to hear the document read, prepared by the committee appointed at the last meeting for that purpose.

We the undersigned Roman Catholic Inhabitants of (8) St. John, New Brunswick, have with much concern lately learned the trials and afflictions of our much revered and esteemed pastor the Rev. CHARLES FFRENCH, whose talents and piety we always admired, and whose almost unexampled zeal for the good of Religion during his stay amongst us characterised him as a Christian Priest. To his exertions we are indebted for our Church, to procure money for the building of which as well as other Churches in this Province, he undertook laborious journies and perilous voyages. The monies collected through him were expended on our Church with strict economy, and scrupulous exactness, as it appears from the report of the Committee appointed at his own request, to inspect the Chapel accounts during the whole time of his administration, and which is fully stated in the Gazette of St. John, bearing date the 19th February, 1817.

But whereas the voice of calumny endeavoured to cloud such exalted worth, it becomes therefore the duty of every lover of truth and justice to repel the foul and sacreligious attempt.

It is only lately we have discovered the poisonous source from whence it flowed, from a man by name Richard Toole, on whose testimony the smallest reliance cannot be placed, being a man of foul character, and prone to intemperance and unblushing immorality, such is his well known character, which can be attested by several persons in this City, should the same be required. *This is the man* as we are informed, who had the audacity to address the most Rev. Bishops of Quebec, and New-York, on a subject of infamy and falsehood ! ! !

We beg leave to express the high opinion we entertain of and the unshaken confidence we have in the Rev. CHARLES FFRENCH, and we prize as a certain blessing his visit to our City. We beg him to accept of our unalterable esteem, and of unfeigned thanks, for the invaluable services he has done for us.

The following resolutions were then proposed and unanimously carried.

Appendix A. *A Short Memoir* 167

(9) Resolved 1st. That we highly approve of this document, that it expresses our sentiments, and that all here present do affix our signatures thereto.

Resolved 2dly. That a Committee of three be appointed by the Chairman to procure signatures of such of the congregation as are absent, and afterwards to enclose the document together with the resolutions of this meeting signed by the Chairman and Secretary, and present the Rev. CHARLES FFRENCH with the same in a most respectful manner.

The chairman them [sic] named the three following gentlemen, as the Committee, Mr. Thomas Waters, Mr. Patrick Murphy, Mr. Philip Kehoe.

(Signed)   WM. CUMMINS, Chairman.
                                  PHILIP KEHOE, Secretary.

St. John, June 6th, 1821.

SIGNATURES of the Members of the Congregation to the above document.

The former Churchwardens.	*The present Churchwardens.*
JOHN TOOLE,	WILLIAM WATERS,
JOHN SINNOT,	THOMAS WATERS,
BERNARD KEIRNAN,	WILLIAM HALE,
PATRICK MURPHY,	MICHAEL CANTY,
WILLIAM CUMMINS,	JAMES GALLAGHER,
Philip Kehoe,	Thomas Fitzpatrick,
Patrick Cummins,	William Foley,
John Ford,	Thomas Parker,
James Nowlan,	Thomas Gillespie,
John Dooly,	Arthur Quirk,
John M'Carthy,	Bartholemew Buckley,
James Whitty,	John Connolly,
William Whitty,	Edward Roche,
John Dougherty,	Nicholas Wise, Sen.
William Wise,	Nicholas Wise, Jun.
Martin Hayden,	Patrick Furlong,
Peter Hayden,	Philip Furlong,
Michael Murphy,	George O'Brien,
(10) John Griffin,	Charles Wadleton,
John Quin,	Joseph Hoply,

John Sinnot,
Thomas Bean,
John Mullens,
John More,
John Corcoran,
John Codd,
James Codd,
Stephen Murphy,
Stephen Roach,
Andrew Delany,
Patrick Shannon,
James Dowds,
Con. Connolly,
John O'Brien,
John Buckley,
John Lannan,
William Sinnott,
Philip Gallagher,
Maurice Delany,
Dennis Sullivan,
Daniel Sullivan,
Patrick Sullivan,
John Eddy,
John Barry,
Patrick O'Brien,
Michael Burns,
Clement Petit,
Michael Forrestall,
Andrew Power,
Nicholas Wise,
Thomas Owens,
Thomas Wills,
Charles Gallagher,
Charles Waters,
Jeremiah Sullivan, Jun.
Jeremiah Sullivan, Sen.
Owen Dempsey,
(11) Henry O'Neil,
James O'Brien,
Patrick M'Evoy,
William M'Donnell,
Frederick Gaynor,
Arthur Currey,
Thomas Keating,
Robert Sinnot,
Richard Dunn,
Edward Murphy,
Patrick Dunohoe,
William Furlong,
John Furlong,
Patrick Sinnott,
Thomas Coughlan,
Robert Kelly,
John Davis,
Nicholas Scallon,
John Reed,
Martin Murthy,
John Dowling,
Redmond O'Connor,
Mathew Murphy,
John Fitzpatrick,
Thomas Fitzpatrick,
James Kiernan,
John Collins,
Dennis O'Connor,
Thomas O'Connor,
Thomas Mulligan,
James Breen,
Dennis Dunnivan,
Peter Clary,
John Cullen,
Hugh Timmons,
James Kelly,
William Dunn,
Terence Ferguson,
William Downey,
George O'Neil,
William Morrossey,
John Collins,
Michael Kennedy,

James Suillivan,	Michael Sullivan,
John Egan,	James M'Bride,
Jonas Egan,	John O'Connor,

On reading over this document it has excited tears, and all my persecution could not start a single one, but the following letter which I received a day or two after afforded me increased pleasure. It needs no comment.

St. John, June 12th 1822.

REVEREND SIR,

Can I ever expect forgiveness for what I have done; but let me assure your Reverence, the fault was not a free act of mine, it was that unfortunate Toole, who forced me to injure your Character. I presume to send these few lines which are to be handed to you by my daughter Eliza; she kneels in supplication of her mother's forgiveness. I have written last Thursday two letters, one to the Bishop of Canada and another to the Bishop of New-York; in these letters I have contradicted the falsehoods which have been advanced in my several letters to them, the copies I retain, which you can have if you wish. Rev. Sir, I am miserable and can only shew forth my sorrow, in my readiness to do all in my power, to repair the injuries I have done to you and your character. I remain with high respect, your humble and afflicted servant, MARY TOOLE.

I immediately sent for a Copy of the letters which she dispatched to Canada and New-York. My suspicions were well grounded of *a plot.* In these letters she says to the Bishops of Quebec and New-York, *"It was said some person from New-York who was an enemy to Mr. Ffrench bribed him"* (her husband Richard Toole) to injure Mr. FFRENCH'S character.

I also sent to her for a certificate, stating the reasons (**12**) that led her to injure my character before the Bishops of Canada and New-York, and her signature to it, to be witnessed by two respectable householders in this City; she has done so, the following is a copy of it:

I the undersigned do hereby certify the truth of which I am ready to make on oath, that my husband Richard Toole, on several occasions, threatened to molest and take away my life, holding at the same time a knife in his hand to murder me if I refused to write several letters to the Bishops of Canada and New-York, setting forth scandalous falsehoods, injurious to the character of the Rev. CHARLES FFRENCH, in order to injure him in their opinion, and to induce the Bishop of New-York in whose Diocess [sic] he then resided to disgrace him, and deprive him of his living. Moreover I certify that I have forwarded a letter to each of those most Rev. Bishops bearing date the 6th inst. stating the matter to them as I have hereabove declared.

 (Signed)   MARY TOOLE.

St. John, June 14th, 1822.

We the undersigned certify the above signature, together with the instrument also, to be the hand writing of Mary Toole, alias Wills.

           WINIFRED FLOOD,
           THOMAS WATERS.

 I now come to the last charge of my accusers of New-York. It refers to Nancy Mossroll, of Bay-de-wind, Miramichi, who had a child in April, in the year 1817; it was about that time twelve months, that I made my last visit to that place, from whence I went to Nigawick, (the Bay divides both places,) where I stopped a great part of May. I had now finished all my visits to the several parts of my mission, and was preparing to quit Miramichi, to go to the States to get some relief from the Rheumatism which deprived me of walking for some weeks, occasioned by falling through the ice the last winter. I went from Nigawick direct to the mission where I appointed that time to meet with James (**13**) Stack and Hugh Magennis, whom I employed to build the Stone work of Indian Church in Miramichi. I was obliged to stop there from the latter end of May or the beginning of June to the September following, the said Stack and Magennis and his wife lived in the same house with me the entire of that period, during which I was not absent even a day. Now the matter involves this difficulty, I must either cross the Bay where the said Nancy Mossroll was, or she must come to the place where I was, the former could not happen without the knowledge of the said Stack and Magennis; neither could the latter, without the knowledge of the persons who conducted her, and also of the said Stack and Magennis. In September I quit for good Miramichi, and was escorted several miles on my journey by the said James Stack. It was nearly 8 months after this time the said Nancy Mossroll had said child. The truth of all this statement was certified on oath by the said James Stack before Mr. Swanton, Judge in the marine court and notary in New-York. I have lost the certificate in the shipwreck, but I left a copy of it in the hands of the Bishop of New-York. The said Stack was well known by the Rev. Mr. Laracy late of Boston, and by the Rev. Mr. Morisset the Canadian Clergyman, who succeeded me in my mission of Miramichi and who is now the actual Pastor of St. John; both speak highly in favour of him, (said Stack), as a man of excellent good character, and as such should be believed upon his oath. This being premised–

I commenced my long and painful journey to the river of Miramichi; the Catholics along that extended Settlement are Scotch and Irish. The settlements of Bay de wind and Nigawick are all French–on my arrival I found all my old parishoners [sic] enthusiastically glad to see me, some of the French received me on their knees with tears of joy, and the poor Indians of the mission ran in crowds to the shore and saluted me agreeable to their custom with discharges from their fusils, then they conducted me to the Church to offer (**14**) thanks for my arrival, and supplicated me to remain always with them. As for Nancy Mossroll, she was confronted in my presence; her neighbours of Bay de wind told me she was a woman of bad character, that she had several children by different persons (who are now known) before she was married, and they are of opinion that she must be either influenced by some enemy to speak of me as she did, or she had engaged in it, as a design or scheme to get money. I could scarcely withhold them from pouring imprecations on her and on the persons who dared to meddle with my character. In vindication of which I was presented with the following documents, by the venerable John English, Esq. who is a great benefactor of the Church.

We the undersigned Catholic Inhabitants of Miramichi beg leave to congratulate our antient [sic] dear and worthy Pastor Rev. CHARLES FFRENCH on his safe arrival in this settlement, and to express our warmest wishes and our anxious hopes in enjoying the happiness once more of our having him as our Pastor.

We can with truth assert there never was a Clergyman here who has done so much good as he has; only for him we would not have so many new Churches of our communion in this and the neighbouring settlements, particularly the beautiful stone Church at the mission, for the building of which, he underwent incredible labour and fatigue. We beg leave to assure his Reverence of our high opinion of his worth and our sincere esteem for him. His uniform conduct, his unostentatious piety will always ensure the love of those who know him. We feel happy in assuring his Reverence, and which is a consolation, we offer him for the perplexities he has suffered from bad minded persons, that the report, which the tongue of slander endeavoured to obtain belief for, was only believed by a few, we never gave any credit to it, and now there is scarcely any person who would ever speak of it, since certain circumstances have come to light, but as a matter of im- **(15)** position and fraud. May the great God preserve his Reverence in future from the tongue of calumny and from its malicious effects.

John English,	James Davidson,	Bryan Dunn,
William Gordon,	Alexander Davidson,	William Guellis,
George Murdock,	James Davidson, jun.	Martin Walsh,
John Stromach,	Peter Taylor,	John Walsh,
James Stromach,	Peter Taylor, junr.	John Power,
Pat Taylor,	John Taylor,	John Power, junr.
George Taylor,	Andrew Hay,	George Sutton,
George Taylor, jun.	John Hay,	James Sutton,
Peter Taylor,	Andrew Hay, junr.	John Dunn, junr.
James Innis,	William Hay,	William Balden,
Robert Innis,	Daniel Ross,	James Balden,
James Gordon,	James Murdock,	John Balden,
Barthw. Malcom,	Hector M'Kenna,	John Gillice,
John Malcom,	Samuel Waddleton,	James Maher,
Randle Davidson,	Saml. Waddleton, jr.	David Shaughnessy.
Charles M'Donald,	Daniel O'Kief,	
James Inglis,	John Dunn,	

The following document was handed me by Otho Robisheaux, Esq. a most respectable gentleman and a long time justice of the Peace.

We the undersigned French Inhabitants of Bay de Nigawick, and Bay de wind unite in sentiments with those of Miramichi regarding the Rev. CHARLES FFRENCH, we always did, and do now entertain a very high opinion of him as a good and pious priest.

As for the tongue of slander it did not prevail with us, we never believed the malicious and lying report. May God forgive the authors of it. The Rev. CHARLES FFRENCH'S conduct while amongst us was truly pious, regular and exemplary.

Otho Robisheaux,	Michel Allain, junr.	Oliver Robisheaux,
Michel Allain,	Pierre Alain,	Joseph Robisheaux,

Appendix A. *A Short Memoir* 173

Luis Allain,	Michel Tebodo,	Bruno Poirir,
		Nigawick, July 8, 1822.
Joseph Tebodo,	Raphael Casi,	Joseph Doucett,
Guilbert Mossroll,	Placid Casi,	John Nowlan,
Lasan Mossroll,	Pierre Hiber,	Pierre Henri,
Alexis Mossroll,	Francis Martain,	Baptist Dagle, *Capt.*
Jean Casi,	Dominick Martain,	*Militia.*
Jean Casi, junr.	Francois Doucett,	Alexander M'Donald,
David Mossroll,	Alexr. M'Donald,	*Major of Militia.*
		Bay de wind, July 14, 1822.

(16)[In] overhauling and unravelling such a disagreable [sic] subject in all its windings, it must have been painful as you may conceive to my feelings in several instances. I was not led to it by sentiments of anger nor revenge, indeed my enemies and accusers excite rather *my pity*. I often supplicate Heaven for their pardon and forgiveness. The motives that led me to vindicate my character, were in my opinion obligatory; I looked on it as a duty which I owed not only to myself but to the Catholic Community at large; a duty I owed to my family and my Country, and above all a duty I owed to my Religion which has often suffered by the busy and ruthless tongue of slander, through the faults, whether real or imaginary of her Ministers.–Were it not for these motives I would be silent, and leave my cause in the hands of that great Being who is to judge us all one day. Little did I suppose when I left my native country in pursuit of religious enterprise, with a character irreproachable and spotless, after spending the chief years of my life in peace and happiness among a virtuous circle of respectable relatives and friends who held me in veneration and esteem, what anxieties and troubles I was to undergo in these Cantons and Countries from the edge of censure and the sting of malevolence. But now I have discovered the error of this illusion; no person should promise himself an exemption from crosses and persecutions, much less should the ministers of God. Christ the divine model of all perfection, has assured them "he would send them as sheep among wolves; they would be persecuted, calumniated, and despised"–this is the portion of the bitter cup of his afflictions which he hath bequeathed as an inheritance to his followers here below. He himself drank deeply of it, even to its very dregs. "He was truly a man of affliction and sorrow." I shall conclude begging of the great God through the intercession of his only and beloved Son the Lord Jesus, to grant us all grace practically to display in our lives the maxims of the Gospel we profess, and to establish the empire of his Love in all hearts. Permit me dear and beloved brethren to subscribe myself

Your faithful humble servant,
CHARLES FFRENCH.

ST. JOHN, NEW-BRUNSWICK,
    5TH AUGUST, 1822.

Appendix B

(1)   **The Conversion of Charles Ffrench to the Catholic Church**[1]

(2)

(3) The writer of the following memoir was requested on his arrival at Rome, by a very respectable personage, to write the particulars of his Conversion, to the Catholic Church, and the beneficial effects of his ministry as missionary, during a residence of nearly thirty years in North America. He had been hitherto oftentimes solicited by his friends in that quarter, to publish in pamphlet form, his conversion, but he declined it, through motives of delicacy. He was apprehensive, least it might be viewed by the world, as done from vanity, and it would consequently injure, rather than serve, the cause of religion. He now yields to the kind suggestions of him whom he holds in profound veneration, and he gives it in simple and unvarnished language to the world.

Charles D. Ffrench

Dated at Rome
Ap^l. 26. 1840

---

[1] The "Conversion," which is in Ffrench's own handwriting, is transcribed as faithfully as possible given the age and condition of the document, except that capitals have been placed at the beginning and periods at the end of all sentences. No attempt has been made to correct or modernize the spelling or other punctuation. The narrative is not divided into paragraphs. The numerals in bold-face type in the transcription indicate the beginning of a new page. The original document is housed in the Archives of San Clemente in Rome (SCAR, file 28 doc. 62a). The photocopy from which this transcription was made was obtained from the archives of the Dominican Province of Saint Joseph, Providence College, Providence, Rhode Island. An abridged and edited version, entitled "The Conversion of Charles Ffrench," was published by Hugh Fenning O.P. in *The Watchman* 28: 53 (Summer 1961), 34-39.

(4) I was born in the City of Galway, which is the capital of the province of Conought in the west of Ireland, in the year of our Lord 1775, of Protestant parents. My Father was a Prelate of the Church of England, and my mother was the daughter of a distinguished dignitary of the same Church. I had two Brothers and two Sisters. I have only one Brother living who is a Catholic Bishop. The Lord made me the instrument of his conversion and of my eldest Brother, who died at the age of twenty five. My living Sister is a Catholic, the other died when a child of three years of age. I may trace my conversion to a seeming trifling circumstance, but unsearcheable are the ways of God. The circumstance was, on a Sunday morning when a child of between four and five years of age I observed one of the servant women who was preparing to go to mass. I asked her what place was mass. It is a beautiful place said she. (5) I asked her to let me go with her. She told me no, that she dare not. I followed keeping behind her at some distance, least she might notice me but I hastened towards her on her entering the Chapel, and I took her by the hand. She seemed displeased, and desired me to return home, but I was too much pleased with the appearance of the place, to quit it. The altar and the paintings attracted my notice. I viewed with eyes of wonder and astonishment the vestments of the Clergyman who officiated but when the tones of the organ struck my ears, I was very much delighted, and more so with the harmonious voices of the Choir. On seeing the people on their knees I knelt down by the side of the Servant. I pulled her by the cloak, and asked her to tell me, what shall I do? She said, repeat the Our Father. I (6) instantly joined both hands, and said it. I asked her again, what else shall I do? Repeat the Our Father, and I believe in God said she. I accordingly said the Lords prayer and the Apostles Creed. When the mass was finished, and the people were quitting the Chapel, I wished to stop longer, but the Servant called me to come home. I cried out no, I do not want to go. She was oblidged to take me by force in her arms. I sobed for some time, I got out of humour, and I was not easily appeased. On our way home, she cautioned me not to tell where I had been. I asked why? Because said she, I will be bleamed, and it is likely, I shall lose my place. But it was useless to put a padlock on my lips, I could not be silent on the subject. I told every one I met of the affair when I came home, and after dinner I interrupted the conversation of the Company, by telling my Father saying Pa, I saw a beautiful place this (7) morning. He was so much engaged in conversation, that he did not heed me. I then sat upon his knees, and put my hands on his face,

saying Pa, I saw a beautiful place this morning. By this means, I arrested his attention, and that of the entire Company. What place was it my son? O Pa, I stole after Ellenor. I overtook her as she entered the beautiful place, then I took her by the hand, and I went in. But my son tell me, what place must it be that appeared to you so beautiful? O I forget the name of it Pa, but Ellenor can tell you. O now I remember, she called it mass. He smiled, and said, do not go there again. All the company appeared very grave, and I overheard my father say, on my quitting the dining room, He is a very curious child. This entire transaction is as fresh this day in my memory, as if it happened yesterday. (8) At this period I speak of, my Brother and I were under the care of our Grand aunt, the sister of Parson Ireland, for our mother was dead nearly four years, and she died a Catholic. What an extraordinary grace the Lord in his mercy bestowed on her, for she never had any opportunity of knowing any thing of the C. Church. My father married her at the age of fourteen years and seven months, as I have learned. She died rather suddenly, at the age of twenty one. I hope she corresponded fully to Gods grace. May she rest in peace. The Clergyman who attended her was the only surviving witness of the transaction, when he told it to me. He was absent on the continant for many years and he happened to return, much about the time, I returned from Portugal, after my studies. When I was introduced to him, the day after my arrival, the first word he said, O you have a strong resem(9) blance to your mother, or rather an ordinary resemblance to her, for she was reckand to be the prettiest Lady in the entire province. I have no recollection of her said I, for I was only nine months old when she died. But I recollect her well, said he and I attended her on her death bed. You would never know it, only that Providence preserved my life, to assure you of the truth of what I tell you. O Doctor Bodkin do tell me, I am impatient to hear the particulars of it. I always heard she died suddenly. Well then I shall satisfy you. You must know y^r. mother was very fond of attending the assemblies or soirees. She returned home from one of them very ill, a Saturday morning, at one oclock. She complained to her mother, who was on a visit with her, that she was so ill that she did not expect to live two hours and something struck her. (10) She would like to have a visit from a Catholic Clergyman. The mother got angry with her, followed her to her bed chamber, telling her she would wake up one of the Servants, to go for Parson Cambul for her. She cried out O no mother, I will not have him. It is my dying request, that you will send for a Priest. Your Father was in his study room preparing his Sermon. He overheard the conversation. He asked what was the matter? tell me calling your mother by her name Dear Ann. What is the matter with you? She said I want a Priest. He replied by all means, I will go myself for him. You shall have your request. He came himself for me. I gave her all the sacraments wch she received with great piety, and she died a short time afterwards. It may be very well conceived, that this communication was to me a joyful one. I said mass (11) for her eternal repose the next morning. But to resume my short sketch or history, our Grand aunt taught us our prayers and our catechism. She was a strict protestant, but very liberal, and God made me the instrument of her conversion on my return home from College together with four or five of my family as will appear in its proper place. When my Brother and I were old enough to go to a public school our Father consigned us to the care of a Doctor Shaw a protestant minister. Under him we were taught our humanity. He set apart a day in the week for the reading of English history, and scripture. He impressed on our minds, the dignity of the Protestant religion, and the necessity of so glorious a reformation, as that of the 16. century. (12) His manners were mild and very prepossessing. He was loved by every one of his pupils. He was in the opinion of all protestants, a very moral, religious, good man. As for myself, I thought he arrived at the very summit of perfection, and that no person was superior to him in goodness and virtue. Our Father died in 1786. I was then eleven, and my Brother Edmond twelve years of age. Parson Shaw did not desert us in our orphanage. He redoubled his care of us. He behaved as a father to us. It would appear that such attentions working on minds full of sensibility would form a strong barrier to our conversion to the catholic Church. We had no acquaintance with any Catholics until I was about fourteen when an incidence occured simular to that of the first, which I spoke of, when not five years old, and which confirmed the impression I then received, and which brought me and my Brother to a perfect (13) determination of investigating religion, which eventuated in our embracing the faith of J. Christ. The incidence was, I happened to call on our Taylor on Christmas Eve to know whether my new Cloths, and those of my Brother Edmond were made, as we intended to appear in them at Church the next day. Three persons came in just at the time, I was telling the Taylor not to disappoint us. They asked him to go to the midnight mass. I asked him was he a Catholick? Yes said he. I was once said I at mass when a Child, and it made so great an impression on me that I would like most dearly to go, but the difficulty is, how I shall

Appendix B. The Conversion of Charles Ffrench 179

contrive to steal out, without alarming the family. I will go in time said he, and remain opposite the house. You will see me, the moon will shine bright and I will conduct you to the parish Chapel. I kept awake, and, when I saw him, I gently unlocked the door, and decended to the street. The Chapel was not far distant from us, and when I entered it, I was much pleased. The solemn hour of the night, the altar and the entire Chapel was beautifully illuminated (14) and ornamented with flowers and with tufted branches of ever green. The tout ensemble contributed to inspire me with veneration and respect for the house of the Lord. I cannot express what I felt when I viewed the Congregation on their knees, who seemed absorbed in devotional feeling, but when the ministers surrounded the altar, the scene produced a prodigious effect on me. I thought Heaven opened itself to my view. I immediately knelt down and offered something like the following short, but fervent prayer, O Father of heaven! open my eyes to see the truth, grant me thy grace. I humbly beseech thee to do whatever may conduce to thy honor and to follow thee inserably, Amen. After keeping my eyes riveted for some time on the ground, I cast them upwards and I beheld a large Crucifix wch surmounted the frontispiece of the altar, and it was the first that I recollected to have seen. It was as large as life, and well executed in plaster of Paris. I burst into tears, and exclaimed, what a striking (15) representation of my crucified redeemer. I then repeated the Creed and meditated on the forth article "Suffered under Pontius Pilate, was crucified dead and buried." It appeared to me very strange, that my religion did not represent in like manner the great mistery of attonement. Whatever prejudices that I enbibed from my friend Parson Shaw, seemed in a moment to lose their influence on my mind. After the divine Service was over, I hastened home, and I retired to bed. I was so full with reflections, on what I saw, that I could not sleep. Everything passed, and repassed in beautiful imagery before me, until I was summoned to the morning prayer. After breakfast my Brother Edm^d and I were desired to get ready and go to Church Service. On our way, I told him, I had something very important to communicate to him, after the Service. It appeared to me very uninteresting. I longed for the conclusion of it. After which, (16) I proposed to my Brother a long walk to the Country. The day was very fine for the Season of the year, and when we were out of the Town, I disclosed to him (in great Secrecy) my midnight adventure. What said he to me is that the important matter you had to communicate? O! I see you are beginning to lose your senses, but what Charles bewitched you, (said he) to put your foot into a popish Chapel? You are on the way to ruin. Your family will despise you. Every person of sound judgment will also despise you, and justly, for you are shutting the door against all your future prospects and agrandizements in life. He entertained the notion of shortly entering Trinity college and of becoming a minister. I found him so full of these ideas, that I almost relinquished the hopes of bringing him to think as I did, but I did not give him up. I always had great influence on him. After several days conversation on (17) the subject, he appeared to relax a little of that warmth, which in the beginning was rather intense. I constantly importuned him, to come with me to some C. Clergyman for instruction. At length he said I have no objection to become acquainted with the principles of the C. Religion, but for me to go to be instructed by a Priest, that I will never do. However, when I least expected it, he mentioned to me one morning, Charles, I thought a great deal of all you told me. Perhaps you are right. Perhaps the Catholic religion is the true one. I will yield to you, and I will go with you to consult a C. Priest. We accordingly were instructed by a Pius, good, and learned Clergyman. He took every pain to ground us well in the principles of the holy religion. He made us commit to memory a large historical catechism and the entire of the Book, called the Catholic Christian instructed. At the end of three years (18) He judged us fit, and he received us into the Church publicly. The matter became the subject of conversation throughout Town and Country. It was then, that we were called on to encounter with many difficulties, and to suffer trying persecutions. The matter was kept until now a secret from our family, but as soon as it came to their knowledge, we were assailed on all quarters. Our Eldest Brother reproached us most bitterly. Our Guardian the Brother of our mother, threatened us with vengeance. But the Lord gave us courage to bear up against the yells, the cries, the entreaties and the tears of a multitude of friends, relations, and acquaintances finding that all their arguments and entreaties were inadequate, to make the smallest impression on our minds. It was considered, that Parson Shaw our master might succeed. He called on us. He was as smooth as oil. He addressed us in soothing and in affectionate language. (19) You are my D^r. children arrived at a proper age, to enter College, to be fitted for the respective professions, to which you have been destined by your worthy Father. He intended you Edmond for the Church, and you Charles for the Law. I am come by and with the desire of y^r. uncle, to make known, (that) it is his request You hold yourselves in readiness to enter without hesitation,

Appendix B. The Conversion of Charles Ffrench 181

Trinity college. We thanked him for the kind concern which he always manifested for us, and beged leave to decline the offer of our uncle as it did not suit us to enter a protestant establishment. Our friend seemed hily disappointed. He did not expect such answers. He pitied us. We were blind to our own interest, and we were ignorant of the misery that awaited us, for your support will be stoped, and you will be turned out paupers on the street. His words were realised, not many days after this communication. They were made acquainted with our intentions of aspiring one day to the Priesthood (20) and they thought that we must now abandon the hope of it for every obstacle was thrown in our way. We were reduced to the necessity of entering mercantile houses, to gain our subsistance. We regretted to lose so much of our youth at a business, we did not propose to ourselves to pursue, but we were raconciled to the will of providence and patiently waited for the favourable moment to quit it. At the present time, things wore a gloomy aspect. France was closed against us. The revolution had just broken out in that Country. The royal College of Maynooth was closed against us, for by a law of the Trustees the Sons of Protestants were inadmissible. We now began to think that perhaps we were not called to the Eclesiastical State, yet to abandon the hope, and of God opening a way for us at one time or other was a consideration that offered a violence to our feelings. It was during these perplexities that I was led by an invisible hand to the very same chapel wch was the first I entered when a (21) Child. I instantly recollected it. The painting, and the peculiar construction of the Tabernacle were familiar to me. It was the Dominican nunnery Chapel. I prayed to God to give me a vocation to become a religious of that order. My Brother was previously disposed to become a Dominican. He begged of me to go with him to the convent of Esker. I unhesitantly agreed, and we served our noviship there, and made our religious profession. From thence we went to Portugal, and made our studies in the College of Corpo Santo Lisbon. I had not been three years there, when the Climate began to disagree with me. I was constantly recommended by the Phycisian of the college, to go to Ireland, and that my native air might reestablish my health. I held out as long as I could, but my complaint assuming a most serious appearance I was oblidged very reluctantly to yield. It was a tryal to me, to quit my only Brother, and my associates, to whom I was much attached. I embarked aboard a vessel (22) bound for London in the year 1801. We were not many days at sea, when our vessel sprung a leake. She was going down. The water was soon over her Cargo. The

Boatswain cried out we had only five minutes to live. The Captain muttered to himself as he went up on deck, that he would like to see his wife and children before he would take his watery grave. He ordered the 10 pieces of brass cannon to be thrown overbord, and then the entire cargo, consisting of fruit and cotton. He kept the hands constantly employed at the pumps, and at bailing the water in buckets out of the hatch ways. They at length got to the breach, and stoped the leake. During all this time I was engaged below, in indeavouring to save the life of a Madam Sealy (from Madeira). She was going to see her Children, who were at London for their education. She was in a faint the most of the time, and were it not for my attention she would be dreadfully wounded **(23)** by pieces of broken bottles, which were dashing up and down on the caban floor occasiond by our wine lockers bursting open. To describe the awful situation we were in during several hours, it would require the pen of an old navigator. The vessel was perfectly waterloged, sunk deep in the water, and the waves were making a fair passage over her. The hands could scarsely keep the deck during the tremendous gale of wind. What rendered the scene truly awful was the darkness of the night, the roaring of the wind through the rigging or cordage, the vivid flashes of lightning, the loud pales of thunder, and the piteous cries of the seamen invoking Heaven for mercy. At this time M^m Sealy came to herself a little. I thought every heel of the vessel was to be our last. I could (as time did not permit) only say a few, but efficatious expressions. She consented to die a Catholic. I was preparing her to receive the absolution. She accompanied me in repeating the acts of faith hope and charity and just as the Confetion and **(24)** an act of contrition was repeated, at the moment, one of the Seamen cried out, *out of danger*. We were miraculously saved. The next morning we were taken prisoners by a Spanish Privateer, and brought into Guarda in Galicia, a province of the north of Spain. We were kindly treated by the Spaniards, and when liberated, we travelled by land to Aporto in Portugal, where we took passage for Portsmouth. Through my travels in England on my way to Ireland, I met with a M^r. Taylor, a rich american merchant. The Lord made me the instrument of his conversion to the true faith. He urged me to go on the American mission. You are calculated to do much good, for I think you would convert my entire nation. I told him I would go there after spending some time in Ireland. My family were my first concern. The first visit I made was to my grand aunt and to an aunt, the sister of my mother. She had her children mostly married and

Appendix B. The Conversion of Charles Ffrench

settled within a few (25) miles of each other. I commenced my mission with them and happily succeeded in bringing them all over to the faith. In fine, during my stay in Ireland, which was about eight years, I brought over a great number in and out of my family to the C. Church. I then turned my thoughts to the Children of the Desert and in 1810 I set out for the great western world. I called at Lisbon to see a rish relative of mine, a Madame Connoly, who was on her death bed. She was charitably inclined, and she left considerable sums of money to Seven Establishments in Galway, to the Dominican Convent, and Dominican Nunnery, to the Franciscan Convent, and Franciscan Nunnery, to the Augustinian Convent and the Augustian Nunnery, also to the Secular priests Chapel besides a large sum of money to be divided among the indigent room keepers. I understand my (26) Brother commenced his Cathedral with the sum sent for the Secular Priests Chapel, and by the aid wch he rec^d from England and Ireland, he completed the building. After having paid the last respect to the mortal remains of Madame Connolly, having procured the leave of the Father Master Provincial of Ireland and the excellent letters of my ever regretted friend Most Rev. Doct. Troy Arch Bishop of Dublin, I embarked for America and landed (after a dangerous voyage of two months) in S^t. John, Capital of the Province of New Brunswick. As soon as I made the Bishop of Quebec acquainted with my arrival he envited me thither and appointed me first vicar. I preached twice every Sunday. My hearers were chiefly protestants. The Protestant Rector got alarmed, and he took the pains of distributing books (among those whom he learned attended my instructions) books that not only grossly, but (27) most impiously misrepresented the doctrines of the *one holy Catholic & apostolic* Church. Two of them, luckily fell into my hands. I brought them to the Pulpit. I refuted them in a course of lectures, for The Lord furnished me with language effectually to plead the cause of his beloved and only Spouse. During the few months that I remained there, I received into the bosom of the Church nearly twenty individuals among whom, some were of the first grade of respectability and fortune. I shall pass over the persecutions I underwent there. My Bishop was constantly anoyed by the troublesome visits of the Protestant Bishop. I got a mission Else where, of three hundred miles in extent reaching from the City of S^t. John to the Settlements of Miramichi river, which empties itself into the gulph of S^t. Laurence. My little flock would not hear of my quitting them. It was a tryal to me, they were mostly my (28) own converts. They visited in a Body on the Bishop to oblige me to remain and finding him unwilling to detain me, they were very much dissatisfied. I endeavoured to allay the feelings, by taking all the blame on myself. I took my leave of them with tears of regret and after a voyage of five or six hundred miles, I landed in my mission. I had field enough here, to exercise my zeal. There were very few Catholics, and they were dispersed in the woods, and along the windings of the rivers. The first thing I did was to divide my district into five posts, and at each of those posts I built a Church and a Presbitere. It would be difficult for me to describe the privations which I underwent, and the hardships wch I indured for several years, to procure means to finish and complete these buildings. I was often times engaged on journeys in a rude and severe clime in which I had to ascend the steep and craggy rocks (29) (for Roads there were none) or make my way through lonely woods, where the bear and other wild beasts would feign dispute a passage with me. Often times I had to sleep in the open air under the Canopy of Heaven, amid the pittings of a snow storm or of the chilling frost. Other times I undertook long and dangerous voyages traversing boisterous Seas but I succeeded. I was furnished with means and my Catholic errections were completed in those places, where there were none before. There were very few Catholics in S^t. John when I commenced the Church there. They amounted only to seventeen individuals. The Congregation now amounts to nearly five thousand. One Church is not sufficient for them, altho it was enlarged by the Rev. M^r. McMahon, a most zealous pious Clergyman. He now recides at Quebec, where he has built a fine Church. When I had formed Congregations at each of my Posts, and began to assume the appearance of a flourishing condition (30) I was oblidged to give up my mission. I got almost entirely paralyzed. I was called to attend a dying man, of a cold dreary night in winter, a distance of twenty miles. The rivers were solidly froze, but unfortunately, I had gone only the one half of my journey when my horse and my self fell through the ice. I had a very narrow escape of being drowned. I was then pretty active and I saved myself, and the poor animal, but I was so chilled with cold, that I had much difficulty, to reach alive, the house of the dying man; a few minutes more abroad would have put an end to my course. Every care was afforded me by the family. I did not get warm that night. I continued paralized for months and in that state, I was often carried like a corps on the shoulders of men to the dying. I should be laid flat on my back on the floor, and with difficulty I could raise my hand, to administer the sacraments. As soon as a Priest (31) was provided, I left the place, to seek some relief in a milder climate, and I settled in New York. In a short time I recovered my health. I found the Churches there, Sunk in debt, and after a little time, I became so popular among the inhabitants, that I raised nine thousand dollars towards liquidating the debts. I did not confine my labours entirely to New York, but with the leave of my Bishop, the Saintly Lord John Connolly, I made incursions into the interior of the States, into those places, where a priest was never before me. I set up at the houses of the ministers, who treated me with hospitality and kindly gave me the use of their Churches to preach. I was the instrument under Heaven, of bringing over to the faith, Several protestant ministers, with their families and many among their congregations. **(32)** In 1822 It became necessary for me to return to New Brunswick. I embarked for that Port, in the Spectator, a large beautiful looking Ship. We were only a few days out when she started her hull in ends. She soon almost filled with water. She had six feet deep of water in her hold. Waves were dashing up and down, and by their rush, they made a terrible and awful noise. All hopes of being saved were now abandoned. I was preparing to meet my fate, with resignation. I was offering a prayer to God, when I was disturbed by the Steward, who called me to come on deck, saying the vessel was just going to capsize. I told him I will go up in one minute. I found the Captain in tears and all the hands stupefied. The vessel was on her beam ends. The weight of the sand ballast was dipping her under. I asked, why not right the vessel by cutting away the masts &? I hunted for the Carpentry Tools, and I prevailed on some of the hands **(33)** to assist me. We cut away the masts and floated them with all the canvass and cordage over board. By this means she shifted her ballast, and she righted. I had my hands full indeavouring to comfort 17 poor steerage passengers. After doing my duty to them, I was so fatigued, that I stretched myself on the Cabin floor, and fell into a sound sleep until it was four oclock a m. I begged of the Captain to lower the Boats, that we might take to them, & save our lives. He thought it was useless, as he lost his long boat, and the two he had, were inadequate to take all in. The Boats however were lowered. He intended to abandon the poor seventeen Steerage passengers to perish. There was a kind of a roof ladder provided to ascend to **(34)** the gunnel of the vessel, and another to decend to the boats. I took possession first, and as I was determined that we should all perish, or be saved, I would not allow any of the hands to decend to the boats until I had first decended the 17 poor passengers, consisting of men, women & young Boys. There was no alternative. There was no time to be lost, the vessel was just dipping under, when we shoved away from her, least we would be swamped, when the vessel was going down. We were surrounded by a thick fog, in an open Sea, far from land, Sea running mountains high, and yet we most miraculously got safe (after 14 hours) on shore at a place called Kingston in Rhode (35) Island. The story of our adventure was told by the Captn the Crew and Passangers, who acknowledged that they all owed their lives to my courage and wonderful presence of mind, when we were in the most iminent danger, & at a time that we had only a few minutes to live. The poor passangers would kneel in the open streets, and over power me with their expressions of gratitude and thanks for saving their lives. After having made my way to S^t. John by a long and circuitous rout, after having adjusted the business that caused me to go there I took a mission from my Lord Benedict Fenwick Bishop of Boston. He had succeeded Lord John Cheverus who died arch Bishop of Baurdau. Bishop Fenwick had but the Church of Boston, and that of Salem in his entire Diociss, and one or two priests. (36) He immediately took four pious promising young men into his house. He educated them, supported and clothed, and taught them a course of Theology, & ordained them Priests. They are the ornaments of the priesthood. He enlarged his Cathedral. He built an other beautiful Church in Boston, and three or four more in the vicinity. He encouraged active and zealous priests to come and labour in his Diociss, so that there are now (in a few years) upwards of thirty large congregations, instead of only the two I mentioned. He gave me a district of nearly three hundred miles, along the Sea board. I divided it into four posts, where I built my Churches, and dwelling houses, for the Priests. The Church of East port is much admired. So is that of Dover but the Portland Church is a curiosity. (37) The beauty of its architecture is much admired. When I commenced my labours, I had very few Catholics in my mission. They could not (however willing) give me much help towards my buildings. I had to travel far and near and to make application to my Protestant Brethren, and they have assisted me very liberally. The Congregations at each of my posts increased rappidly not only from the number of those persons who joined the Church, but also from the influx of those, who emigrated from Europe to America. I could mention many interesting incidents during my long ressidence in North America but this would swell my narrative beyond my intended purpose. I had many obstacles to overcome. I was often assailed by calumny, often in danger of being assassinated. Hords of itinerant preachers were accustomed to go from house to house spreading their dangerous doctrines. Prejudice ran so high in the breasts of some fanatics that it appeared a merit according to their view of things to pursue the missionary with hostile arms, so as to banish him if they could from the face of mankind. But every thing now **(38)** wears a more peaceable aspect. Although the American mission is truly a painful mission, yet the zealous pious Clergyman is consoled at the view of his labours being successful in bringing over to the true faith of Christ hundreds of individuals, and in erecting the cross of the Savior on the ruins of Superstition, error and infidelity. May this short narrative of my conversion to the *one holy Catholic* and *Apostolic Church*, and my labours as Missionary in the Wilds of America, tend to the greater glory of God and to the Salvation of mankind. Such is the humble prayer of him who Signs himself

Charles D. Ffrench
P.G.

American
A missionary, in propa
-gating the faith of J. Christ.

Appendix C

Petition of Charles Dominic Ffrench to
His Holiness Pope Gregory XVI
28 July 1840[1]

Your Holiness,

Fr. Charles Dominic Ffrench of the Order of Preachers, who for thirty years has been a missionary in America, bows before Your Holiness to implore that we tend to the spiritual needs of the faithful in that part of Nova Scotia, which is what the twelfth district is called, situated on the other coast of the Bay of Fundy, before St. John where Yours Truly will establish a College for which permission was received by Your Holiness. The land in this district is extensive and would cover half of Italy, and there are many Catholics. Most of the time they are saddened by the fact that they do not have religious support, and many of them die without having received the Sacrament of Confirmation because Msgr. Fraser the Vicar Apostolic is only rarely able to go there and the residence of the Msgr. Bishop in Antegonish is too distant and difficult to reach. Since the aforementioned District is so large, it could very well accomodate another Vicar Apostolic. Yours Truly implores Your Holiness to establish the post in order to assist the good Catholics who are growing in number and to be able to send students to the new College to be ordained. If it is pleasing to Your Holiness, he may be chosen from the Religious Order of the Preaching Friars. Yours Truly with extreme joy in the complete knowledge of being able to promote God's Will.

---

[1] Trans. Cristina Povoledo. A photocopy of the original document, which is in Italian and not in Ffrench's own handwriting, can be found in APF LDNA vol. 4 (1837-1841) pt. 2, fols. 419r-419v.

Appendix D

Details sur la Province de la Nouvelle Brunswick par Fr. Charles Dominique Ffrench ordre des Précheurs[1]

La Province de la Nouvelle Brunswick se trouve entre le Canada vers le Nord, les Etats Unis vers le Sud, la Province de Nova Scotia vers l'ouest, et la Baye de Fundy vers l'Est.

Son etendue depuis le Portage qui la devise du Canada dans la Colonie de Madawaska (qui est le territoire, dont on se dispute dans le moment-ci entre les Etats-Unis et La Grande Bretagne) jousqu'aux frontieres des Etats-Unis, sur la rivière Sainté Croix, est de Sept a huit cents milles romaines en longuer; et depuis la baye de Fundy, par laquelle une grand partie de ses rivages sont lavés, jusqu'a Nova Scotia, est plus de cents mille de largeur, le tout etant ainsi un Pays, à peu près aussi grand que L'angleterre.

Je diviserai cette Province en trois Districts, savoir celui du Nord, celui du milieu, et celui du midi; ainsi qui suit.

District du nord (1er)

Je commence ce district avec la riviere miramichi, qui a Sa Source près de la rivière Nashwalk, et qui apres un cours d'environ 150 milles se perd dans le golfe de St. Laurent, et qui à chaque coté des vastes colonies, et des grandes et petites villes bien peuplées, dans lequelles, un commerce trés etendu est poussé avec l'engleterre et les Indes

---

[1] This document has been transcribed from a photocopy obtained in Rome through the good offices of Fr Theodore Reznowski, without, however, the location of the original being made known to us. The transcription has been done as faithfully as possible, given the document's age, with no attempt made to correct or modernize the spelling or capitalization. A photocopy of a second version of the same document, almost identical to the first but lacking the last two small sections, can be found in APF LDNA, vol. 4 (1837-1841) pt. 3, 517-525. Both documents are apparently in Ffrench's own handwriting.

occidentales, en gros bois, en bois à scier, en saumon, et en la pelleterie. Cette rivière est navigable pour les grands batiments de 600 tonneaux de port, jusqu'a 60 milles de la mer, et pendant une grande partie de l'année, presente le Spectacle d'une fôret de mâts. Ici les Eglises se trouvent à la distance environ de 20 milles l'une de l'autre, et en decendant la riviere de ces endroits, se trouvent l'eglise de Bartabog, et puis Celle des Indiens, puis l'Eglise de Nigaweck & plus bas la rivière se devise en deux bayes, savoir, la baye de Chaleur, et la baye du vent, à l'entrée de la baye de Chaleur on trouve des grandes villes, plaines de Catholiques. Apres d'être eloignè de Tashabontack et Tracady, il y a une grande Eglise à Caraket, lieu très bien peuplés: ensuite le point au Rocher, et puis Ristigoosh, avec une belle Eglise.

À l'entrée de la baye du vent il y a deux grandes Colonies, qui portent ce nom, et qui sont pleines d'habitants; et plus loin il y a deux autres Colonies très grandes et bien peuplés (avec deux Eglises) qu'on appelle Richiboocto; ensuit il y a Cocagne, et puis un grand Colonie ou établisement avec une jolie Eglise à Bucktoosh; mais depuis cet endroit la population est légèrement semée jusqu'a Shediack, avec lequel, Ici commencerai le district du Midi.

Le nombre des Eglises en ce district (du nord) est vingt.

Ce District offre un champ assez grand pour l'exercise du zèle missionaire: et si quelqu'un, en même temps habile et actif pouvait être trouvé pour le gouverner, Combien s'étenderait, en peu de temps l'empire de la religion! Peutêtre Monsr. l'evêque Hines, qui n'est pas, je crois, engagè dans ce moment-ci dans les soins d'aucune diocèse, et qui est un excellent missionaire, pouvait être persuadé à ce propos. En general je puis dire, pour tous les Districts, que l'établisement des Ecoles dans chaqu'un deux, avec des maitres bien choisis pour sourveiller à l'education de la jeunesse protestante aussi bien que Catholique, serait plus efficase qu'aucune autre chose à catholiser le pays.

Moi même j'en a fait l'expérience, à S^t. Jean, et bientôt 70 enfans protestants furent confiés à mes soins. Le consequence est evident. aussi il serait très à desirer que l'evêque pourait visiter souvent tous les endroits dont Je fais mention, parceque il arrive toujours qu'à l'occasion de ces visites les protestants courent en foule pour entendre les paroles de la vie de sa bouche.

District au milieu
(2^{ime})

Je Commence avec Fredericton, une grand et opulent ville, et la siege du governement; ici il y a une Eglise, et une Congregation Catholique de plus de 1000. La ville est bâtie sur les bords de la riviere S^t. Jean, qui a sa source au dessus des fourches de la riviere Madawaska, et s'ecoule 500 milles jusqu'à son embouchure dans la baie de Fundy, pres de la ville de S^t. Jean. Fredericton est situè à 400 milles de la source de ce fleuve, et à cent milles de la ville de S^t. Jean; la largeur du fleuve varie d'une demi-mille à deux milles, et il y a plusieurs belles colonies et etablisements magnafiques sur ses deux bords, jusqu'à Madawaska, mais les Catholiques ne sont pas nombreux jusqu'à cette même Colonie de Madawaska, qui est très peuplée, et dont les habitants sont presque tous Français, ayant plusieurs belles Eglises. Ensuite revenant par la même riviere à Fredericton, et descendant jusqu'à Major-field.[2] On trouve plusieurs Colonies mais les Catholiques en sont en petit nombre, quelques Centaines, par example qui sont pour le plus part ou Francais ou Indiens. Ici est terminé le district du milieu, dont le nombre des Eglises est 12.

District du Midi (3me)

Je Commence avec la ville de S^t. Jean, assise sur la baye de Fundy, une grande ville, très peuplée et opulente; et la Capital de la province avec 5000 Catholiques et une Eglise magnifique.

De S^t. Jean à S^t. André le long de la baye de Fundy, environ 90 milles, les Catholiques sont très nombreux, surtout à Carleton, Macadavid et à S^t. André qui est une ville considerable, et ou il y a une belle petite eglise, le nombre des Catholiques ne monte à plus de 600: et plus loin, jusqu'aux frontiers des Etats unis, il y a environ 60 milles, et dans cette etendue les Catholiques sont parsemés ça et là, mais pas en grand nombre, jusqu'à Calais, qui est sur les frontieres de deux nations, et on se trouve une Eglise, et une population d'environ 500 Catholiques.

De S^t. Jean à Majorfield il y a quelques Catholiques dispersés, et puis en ascendant la riviere Kenebeccasis il y a Hampton-Ferry, Sussex

---

[2] Maugerville, as Ffrench's "Major-field" is now known, is the second oldest English settlement in the colony of New Brunswick.

vale, et Pedigodiack, qui est à environ de 120 milles de S^t. Jean. Ensuite on trouve peu de Catholiques jusqu'à ce qu'on vient à Memoramcook et Shediack, deux grandes Colonies Francaises bien peuplées avec au moins, 2000 Catholiques, et qui forment les limites du 3me District. Il y a 4 ou 5 eglises.

1er District

La Province de nova Scotia est sous la jurisdiction de Monsr. Fraser vicaire apostolique de Halifax & qui peut y aller très rarement. Il a fait sa residance à Antigonish qui est un très grand distance de Halifax. Iici il y a un territoire bien suffisent pour un District integral.

2me District

Dans cette province, il y a de Halifax jusqu'aux limites de Nova Scotia les grandes jurisdictions de Windsor, de Horton, de Conwallis, de Grenville etc. et dans tout ce vaste pays, il y a un grand nombre de Catholiques, Mais à present ils peuvent jouir d'une visite de leur Evêque tres rarement. Ce teritoire est au moins aussi grand que L'Italie entiere, et qui contient aussi partout des grand villes et ports de mer comme Digby, Anapolis Royal, Plymout, Shelburn & enfin cette partie de Nova Scotia qui est située à l'autre coté de la baye vis à vis de S^t. John d'ou la traversée est fait par des bateaux à vapeur en 2 au 3 heurs, formerait d'elle même un territoire assez grand pour un vicaire apostolique.

Il y a environ 4 Eglises.

BIBLIOGRAPHY

Acheson, T.W. *Saint John: The Making of a Colonial Urban Community.* Toronto: University of Toronto Press, 1985.

Allaire, Jean-Baptiste-Arthur. *Dictionnaire biographique du clergé canadian-français.* Vol. 1, *Les Anciens.* Montreal: Imprimerie de l'Ecole catholique des sourds-muets, 1910.

American Catholic Historical Researches 8: 1 (Jan. 1891), 67, Ffrench to Conwell (New York, 7 Feb. 1822).

Barbour, Daniel. *The History of My Own Times.* Washington, D.C., 1828.

Bayley, James R. *A Brief Sketch of the Early History of the Catholic Church on the Island of New York.* 2nd ed. New York: New York Catholic Publication Society, 1870.

Boston Pilot, March 1851. "The Late C.D. Ffrench."

Boyle, Leonard E. San Clemente Miscellany I The Community of SS Sisto e Clemente in Roma (Rome: S. Clemente, 1977).

Brasseur de Bourbourg, Charles Etienne. *Histoire du Canada, de son église et de ses missions.* 2 vols. Paris: Sagnier et Bray, 1852. Reprint: East Ardsley, Wakefield: S.R. Pubs, 1968.

Byrne, Cyril, ed. *Gentlemen-Bishops and Faction Fighters: Letters of Bishops O Donel, Lambert, Scallan and Other Irish Missionaries.* St. John's: Jesperson Press, 1984.

Byrne, William, et al. *History of the Catholic Church in the New England States.* 2 vols. Boston: Hurd & Everts, 1899.

Carey, Patrick. "The Laity's Understanding of the Trustee System, 1785-1855." *Catholic Historical Review* 64: 3 (1978), 357-376.

Carey, Patrick W. "Lay Leadership in Catholic Parishes." *New Catholic World* 228 (Nov.-Dec. 1985), 279-281.

Carey, Patrick W. *People, Priests, and Prelates: Ecclesiastical Democracy and the Tensions of Trusteeism*. Notre Dame: University of Notre Dame Press, 1987.

Carey, Patrick W. *The Roman Catholics*. Westport, Conn.: Greenwood Press, 1993. Denominations in America no. 6.

Caron, Ivanhoë. "Mgr Joseph-Octave Plessis, Archevêque de Québec, et les Premiers Evêques Catholiques des Etats-Unis." *Mémoires de la Société Royale du Canada*, 3rd series, 28 (1934), 119-138.

Chassé, Sonia. "Signay, Joseph." In *Dictionary of Canadian Biography* VII (1836-1850), 798-800.

City Gazette [Saint John], 1 May 1822; 2 Dec. 1824.

Codignola, Luca. "L'Amérique du Nord et la Sacrée Congrégation 'de Propaganda Fide', 1622-1799–Guides et Inventaires." *Revue d'Histoire de l'Amérique Française* 33: 2 (Sept. 1979), 197-214.

Codignola, Luca. *L'Amérique du Nord française dans les archives religieuses de Rome, 1600-1922: Guide de recherche*, sous la direction de Pierre Hurtubise, Luca Codignola et Fernand Harvey. Sainte-Foy: Éditions de l'IQRC, 1999.

Codignola, Luca. "Conflict or Consensus? Catholics in Canada and in the United States, 1780-1820." CCHA *Historical Studies* 55 (1988), 43-59.

Codignola, Luca. "The Policy of Rome towards the English-Speaking Catholics in British North America, 1750-1830." In *Creed and Culture: The Place of English-Speaking Catholics in Canadian Society, 1750-1930*, eds. Terrence Murphy and Gerald Stortz (Montreal & Kingston: McGill-Queen's University Press, 1993), 100-125.

Coen, Martin. *The Wardenship of Galway*. Galway: Kenny's Bookshop & Art Gallery, 1984.

The Columbian [New York], 30 July 1819. "Interesting Law Case. Mayor's Court. Charles Ffrench vs Lewis Willcocks."

Connolly, Sean J. *Priests and People in Pre-Famine Ireland.* New York: St. Martin's Press, 1982.

Cooney, Robert. *A Compendious History of the Northern Part of the Province of New Brunswick and of the District of Gaspé in Lower Canada.* Halifax: [J. Howe], 1832.

Corrigan, Michael Augustine. *Historical Records and Studies* 2 (1901), 40-42. *Register of Clergy.* Ffrench, Rev. Charles Dominic, O.S.D.

Dictionnaire biographique des évêques catholiques du Canada: les diocèses catholiques canadiens des Eglises latine et orientale et leurs évêques; repères chronologiques et biographiques, 1658-2002. Ottawa: Wilson & Lafleur, 2002.

Dignan, Patrick Joseph. *A History of the Legal Incorporation of Catholic Church Property in the United States (1784-1932).* New York: P.J. Kenedy & Sons, 1935.

Dignan, Patrick Joseph. "Peter Anthony Malou, Patriot and Priest (1753-1827)." *Records of the American Catholic Historical Society of Philadelphia* 42: 4 (Dec. 1931), 305-343; 43: 1 (March 1932), 62-96.

A Dominican Bibliography and Book of Reference 1216-1992: A History of Works in English by and about Members of the Order of Friars Preachers. Compiled by Charles R. Auth O.P. Edited by James R. Emond. General Editor James A. Driscoll O.P., S.T.D. New York: Peter Lang, 2000.

Donnelly, Anna M. "Connolly, John (1747/48 or 1751-1825)." In *Encyclopedia of American Catholic History*, eds. Michael Glazier and Thomas J. Shelley (Collegeville, Minn.: Liturgical Press, 1997), 373-374.

Donnelly, James S. *The Land and the People of Nineteenth-Century Cork: The Rural Economy and the Land Question.* London & Boston: Routledge & Kegan Paul, 1975.

Dwyer, Kevin F., O.S.A. "Robert Browne, O.S.A.'s 1820 Report to Cardinal Fontana on the State of Catholicism in Washington, D.C., Virginia, the Carolinas, Georgia and

Louisiana." *Records of the American Catholic Historical Society of Philadelphia* 103: 1 (Spring 1992), 41-61.

Eastern Argus [Eastport, Maine], 6 Oct. 1838.

Farley, John M. *History of St. Patrick's Cathedral.* New York: Society for the Propagation of the Faith, 1908.

Fay, Terence J. *A History of Canadian Catholics: Gallicanism, Romanism, and Canadianism.* Toronto: McGill-Queen's University Press, 2002.

Fenning, Hugh, O.P. "The Conversion of Charles Ffrench." *The Watchman* 28: 53 (Summer 1961), 34-39.

Fenning, Hugh, O.P. *The Undoing of the Friars of Ireland: A Study of the Novitiate Question in the Eighteenth Century.* Louvain: Bibliothèque de l'Université, 1972.

Ferland, Jean-Baptiste-Antoine. *Mgr. Joseph-Octave Plessis: évêque de Québec.* Quebec: L. Brousseau, 1878.

Fogarty, Gerald P. "Lay Trusteeism: Yesterday and Today." *America* 115: 21 (19 Nov. 1966), 656-659.

Galarneau, Claude. "Demers, Jérôme." In *Dictionary of Canadian Biography* VIII (1851-1860), 210-215.

Gubbins, Joseph. *New Brunswick Journals of 1811 & 1813*, ed. Howard Temperley. Fredericton: New Brunswick Heritage Publications, 1980.

Guilday, Peter. *The Catholic Church in Virginia (1815-1922).* New York: United States Catholic Historical Society, 1924. Monograph Series vol. 8.

Guilday, Peter. *The Life and Times of John England.* 2 vols. New York: America Press, 1927. Reprint: New York: Arno Press and The New York Times, 1969.

Guilday, Peter. *The National Pastorals of the American Church 1792-1919.* Westminster, Md.: Newman Press, 1959.

Guilday, Peter. "Trusteeism." *Historical Records and Studies* 18 (March 1928), 7-73.

Hennessey, Michael F., ed. *The Catholic Church in Prince Edward Island, 1720-1979.* Charlottetown: Roman Catholic Episcopal Corp., 1979.

Hughes, Thomas A. *History of the Society of Jesus in North America*. 3 vols. New York: Longman's, Green & Co., 1908-1917.
Hynes, Leo J. *The Catholic Irish in New Brunswick: A History of their prominent role in the Shaping of the Province and the Structuring of the Roman Catholic Church*, ed. J. Edward Belliveau. Moncton: L. Hynes, 1992.
Jennings, John. *Tending the Flock: Bishop Joseph-Octave Plessis and Roman Catholics in Early 19th Century New Brunswick*. Saint John: Diocese of Saint John, 1998.
Johnston, Angus Anthony. *A History of the Catholic Church in Eastern Nova Scotia*. 2 vols. Antigonish: St. Francis Xavier University Press, 1960-1971.
Kauffman, Christopher J. *Tradition and Transformation in Catholic Culture: The Priests of Saint Sulpice in the United States from 1791 to the Present*. New York: Macmillan, 1988.
Kenneally, Finbar, O.F.M., ed. *United States Documents in the Propaganda Fide Archives. A Calendar*. 12 vols. Washington, D.C.: Academy of American Franciscan History, 1966-1987.
Lambert, James H. "Plessis, Joseph-Octave." In *Dictionary of Canadian Biography* VI (1821-1835), 586-599.
Laurent, Laval, O.F.M. *Québec et l'Eglise aux Etats-Unis sous Mgr Briand et Mgr Plessis*. Montreal: Librairie St. François, 1945.
Lawrence, Joseph Wilson. *Footprints or Incidents in the Early History of New Brunswick*. Saint John: J. & A. McMillan, 1883.
LeBlanc, Ronnie Gilles. "Antoine Gagnon and the Mitre: A Model of Relations Between *Canadien*, Scottish and Irish Clergy in the Early Maritime Church." In *Religion and Identity: The Experience of Irish and Scottish Catholics in Atlantic Canada*, eds. Terrence Murphy and Cyril J. Byrne (St. John's: Jesperson Press, 1987), 98-113.

LeBlanc, Ronnie-Gilles. "Antoine Gagnon et ses paroissiens–les constructions." *Revue de l'université Sainte-Anne* (1987): 74-89.
LeBlanc, Ronnie-Gilles. "Gagnon, Antoine." In *Dictionary of Canadian Biography* VII (1836-1850), 332-333.
Léger, Guy. "L'Eglise de Yarmouth fête ses noces d'argent." *L'Eglise canadienne* 11 (1 June 1978), 601-603.
Lord, Robert H., John E. Sexton and Edward T. Harrington. *History of the Archdiocese of Boston, in the Various Stages of its Development, 1604 to 1943*. 3 vols. New York: Sheed & Ward, 1944.
Lucey, William, S.J. "Charles Ffrench and the Maine Coast." In *The Catholic Church in Maine* (Francistown, N.H.: Marshall Jones & Co., 1952), 65-81.
MacDonald, Allan. "Angus Bernard MacEachern, 1759-1835: His Ministry in the Maritime Provinces." In *Religion and Identity: The Experience of Irish and Scottish Catholics in Atlantic Canada*, eds. Terrence Murphy and Cyril J. Byrne (St. John's: Jesperson Press, 1987), 53-67.
Macdonald, G. Edward. "Macdonald, Bernard Donald." In *Dictionary of Canadian Biography* VIII (1851-1860), 528-530.
Macdonald, G. Edward. "MacEachern, Angus Bernard." In *Dictionary of Canadian Biography* VI (1821-1835), 447-451.
Macmillan, John C. *The Early History of the Catholic Church in Prince Edward Island*. Quebec: Evenement Printing Co., 1905.
Maguire, John Francis. *The Irish in America*. London: Longman's, Green & Co., 1868. Reprint: New York: Arno Press and The New York Times, 1969.
Maréchal, Ambrose. "Account to Propaganda, 16 October 1818." Printed in *Catholic Historical Review* 1 (1915-1916), 439-453.

McAvoy, Thomas T., C.S.C. "The Formation of the Catholic Minority." In *Catholicism in America*, ed. P. Greason (New York: Harper & Row, 1970), 10-27.

McDonald, Walter. *Reminiscences of a Maynooth Professor*. London: J. Cape, 1926.

McNally, Vincent J. "John Thomas Troy, Archbishop of Dublin, and the Establishment of Saint Patrick's College, Maynooth, 1791-1795." *Catholic Historical Review* 67: 4 (1981), 565-588.

McNamara, Robert F. "Trusteeism in the Atlantic States, 1785-1863." *Catholic Historical Review* 30: 2 (July 1944), 135-154.

McNutt, W.S. *New Brunswick: A History, 1784-1867*. Toronto: Macmillan of Canada, 1963.

Melanson, Maurice F. "Antoine Gagnon, prêtre missionnaire et grand vicaire en Acadie (1809-1849)." *La Société historique acadienne* 5 (1974), 161-177.

Melville, Annabelle M. *Lefebvre de Cheverus, 1768-1831*. Milwaukee: Bruce Publishing Co., 1958.

Millman, Thomas R. "Mountain, Jacob," In *Dictionary of Canadian Biography* VI (1821-1835), 523-529.

Murphy, Terrence. "The Emergence of Maritime Catholicism, 1781-1830." *Acadiensis* 13: 2 (Spring 1984), 29-49.

Murphy, Terrence. "Introduction." In *Creed and Culture: The Place of English-Speaking Catholics in Canadian Society, 1750-1930*, eds. Terrence Murphy and Gerald Stortz (Montreal & Kingston: McGill-Queen's University Press, 1993), xvii-xxxix.

Murphy, Terrence. "Trusteeism in Atlantic Canada: The Struggle for Leadership among the Irish Catholics of Halifax, St John's, and Saint John, 1780-1850." In *Creed and Culture: The Place of English-Speaking Catholics in Canadian Society, 1750-1930*, eds. Terrence Murphy and Gerald Stortz (Montreal & Kingston: McGill-Queen's University Press, 1993), 126-151.

Murther, Ronin. "The Life of the Most Reverend Ambrose Maréchal Third Archbishop of Baltimore, 1768-1828." Ph.D. thesis. Catholic University of America, 1965.

New-Brunswick Courier [Saint John], 28 March, 1815; 13 May 1815; 11 Dec. 1824; 28 May 1825; 1 Dec. 1827.

New Catholic Encyclopedia. 2nd ed. 15 vols. Washington, D.C.: Thomson/Gale in association with the Catholic University of America, 2003.

Noiseux, François-Xavier, ed. *Liste Chronologique des évêques et des prêtres tant séculiers que réguliers, employés au service de l'Eglise du Canada depuis l'établissement de ce pays, et aussi la liste des évêques des autres possessions britanniques de l'Amérique du Nord*. Quebec: T. Cary, 1834.

O'Connor, Thomas H. "Cheverus, Jean-Louis (1768-1836)." In *Encyclopedia of American Catholic History*, eds. Michael Glazier and Thomas J. Shelley (Collegeville, Minn.: Liturgical Press, 1997), 324-325.

O'Daniel, Victor Francis. "Appendix E." Unpublished manuscript in the Archives of the Dominican Province of Saint Joseph, Providence College, Providence, Rhode Island.

O'Daniel, Victor Francis. *The Dominican Province of Saint Joseph*. New York: National Headquarters of the Holy Name Society, 1942.

O'Donnell, Patrick D. *The Irish Faction Fighters of the 19th Century*. Dublin: Anvil Books, 1975.

O'Gallagher, Marianna, S.C.H. "Irish Priests in the Diocese of Quebec in the Nineteenth Century." CCHA *Study Sessions* 50 (1983), 403-413.

O'Gallagher, Marianna. "McMahon, Patrick." In *Dictionary of Canadian Biography* VIII (1851-1860), 581-582.

O'Gallagher, Marianna, S.C.H. *Saint Patrick's, Quebec: The Building of a Church and of a Parish 1827 to 1833*. Quebec: Carraig Books, 1981.

Osborne, Arthur M. "Charles Ffrench, Pioneer Missionary." CCHA *Report* 19 (1952): 77-86.
"Peter Ffrench." Compiled by Thompson Cooper, in *Dictionary of National Biography*, VII, 693.
Plessis, Joseph-Octave. *Journal de deux voyages apostoliques dans le golfe Saint-Laurent et les provinces d'en bas, en 1811 et 1812*. Quebec: Le Foyer Canadien, 1865.
Plessis, Joseph-Octave. *Journal des visites pastorales de 1815 et 1816*, ed. Henri Têtu. Quebec: Imprimerie Franciscaine Missionnaire, 1903.
Plessis, Joseph-Octave. *Journal d'un voyage en Europe par Mgr Joseph-Octave Plessis, Evêque de Québec, 1819-1820*. Quebec: Pruneau et Kirouac, 1903.
Pothier, Bernard. "Sigogne, Jean-Mandé." In *Dictionary of Canadian Biography* VII (1836-1850), 800-806.
Power, Thomas P., ed. *The Irish in Atlantic Canada, 1780-1900*. Fredericton: New Ireland Press, 1991.
Rapport de L'Archiviste de la Province de Québec pour 1927-1928. Quebec: Rédempti Paradis, 1928.
Rapport de L'Archiviste de la Province de Québec pour 1928-1929. Quebec: Rédempti Paradis, 1929.
Royal Gazette [Saint John], 29 Aug. 1814.
Ryan, Leo R. *Old St. Peter's: The Mother Church of Catholic New York (1785-1935)*. New York: United States Catholic Historical Society, 1935.
Ryan, Leo R. "Pierre Toussaint 'God's Image Carved in Ebony.'" *Historical Records and Studies* 25 (1 June 1935), 39-58.
Spalding, Thomas W. "Maréchal, Ambrose (1768-1828)." In *Encyclopedia of American Catholic History*, eds. Michael Glazier and Thomas J. Shelley (Collegeville, Minn.: Liturgical Press, 1997), 838.
St. Andrew's Chronicle, 12 March 1841.
Tanguay, Cyprien, ed. *Répertoire général du clergé canadien, par ordre chronologique depuis la fondation de la colonie jusqu'à nos jours*. Montreal: Eusèbe Senécal et fils, 1893.

Têtu, Henri. *Les Evêques de Québec: notices biographiques.* Quebec: N.-S. Hardy, 1889.

Thériault, Léon. "Les Missionnaires et leurs paroissiens dans le nord-est du Nouveau-Brunswick 1766-1830." *Revue de l'Université de Moncton* 9: 1-3 (Oct. 1976), 31-51.

Valigny, Pacifique de, O.F.M. Cap. *Chroniques des plus anciennes églises de l'Acadie.* Montreal: L'Echo de Saint-François, 1944.

Vicchio, Stephen J., and Virginia Geiger S.S.N.D., eds. *Perspectives on the American Catholic Church, 1789-1989.* Westminster, Md.: Christian Classics, Inc., 1989.

Walsh, Louis. S. *Origin of the Catholic Church in Salem.* Boston: Cashman, Keating & Co., 1890.

Zwierlein, Frederick. "Les nominations épiscopales aux premiers temps de l'épiscopat américain." In *Mélanges d'Histoire offerts à Charles Moeller.* 2 vols. (Louvain: Université de Louvain, 1914), vol. 2, 527-555.

Index of Persons and Rural Localities

Antigonish 120
Athenray (Ire.) 25

Bandon (Ire.) 42
Barbour, Daniel 65, 76
Barbour, Virgil 65
Bartibog 13, 35-39, 51-52, 58-60, 63, 99, 135, 140, 152
Bay du Vin 35, 47, 52-53, 97-98, 108
Bear River 121
Beaubien, Jean Louis 71, 75-77
Bonaparte, Napoleon 153
Bourg, Joseph 37
Brasseur de Bourbourg, Charles Etienne 130-133
Browne, Robert 143
Burke, Edmund 62
Burnt Church 35, 51-52, 152

Cannon, Mr 76
Carbry, Thomas 19, 66, 80, 154
Caron, Ivanhoë 154-155
Carroll, John 135
Carroll, John [Archbishop] 144n.33
Carroll, Michael 101-104, 107, 141, 156
Cheverus, Jean-Louis de 63, 87, 93
Chubb, Henry 98
Claremont (U.S.) 65
Codignola, Luca 133, 136, 142, 157
Connolly, John 13-14, 21, 49, 66-78 79-90, 95-96, 101-102, 110, 115, 126, 139, 141, 145-147, 149n.41, 153-155, 157
Connolly, Madame 28n.8
Conwell, Henry 90
Cooke, Thomas 98-99
Cooper, Francis 66, 81, 86, 148n.40
Corrigan, Michael Augustine 126
Coyne, Richard 27-28

Dean, John 37
Demers, Jérôme 131-132
Dignan, Patrick 77, 148
Dollard, William 105-109, 123
Dover (U.S.) 117
Dunphy, James 123-124
Durant, William 37

Eastport (U.S.) 41, 116-117
English, John 97-98
Esker (Ire.) 25
Ewer, Thomas 42-43

Fenning, Hugh 137
Fenwick, Benedict 14, 110, 115-118, 125-126
Ffrench, Baron Thomas 24
Ffrench, Edmund 24-26, 28-30
Ffrench, Edmund, Warden of Galway 23-24
Ffrench, Peter 25
Fitzpatrick, Bernard 126-127, 159
Flanagan, John 42
Flood, Simon 118
Fontana, Francesco 80, 83n.8, 91, 110, 144, 155
Fransoni, Giacomo Filippo 119, 122, 124
Fraser, William 43

Gagnon, Antoine 17, 35-36, 44n.32, 45-48, 51, 53, 134-135, 138
Gallagher, John 125
Gaudet, Placide 151-153
Gibbins, Patrick 30-31
Gregory XVI, Pope 19, 119-120, 124
Griffiths, Mr 105
Griffiths, Mrs 105

Hampton 41

Horsfield, Thomas 37
Hughes, John 126
Huot, François-Mathias 152

Ireland [Ffrench], Ann 24

Jordan, Margaret E. 126

Kehoe, Philip 88
Kennebecasis 37, 61
Kiernan, Bernard 38, 56-57
Kohlmann, Anthony 155

La Marche, Fr 125
Lambert, Patrick 38, 42
Lariscy, Phillip 96
Lartigue, Jean Jacques 90, 137
Laurent, Laval 73, 147, 155-156
Lawrence (U.S.) 117, 125

LeBlanc, Ronnie Gilles 134-135
Lewis, Mr 27

Macchi, Vincenzo 29-31
Macdonald, Bernard Donald 19, 120, 122-125
MacEachern, Angus 44n.31, 47n.40, 112-113, 134-136, 139-140
MacPherson, Paul 113
Madawaska 33, 55, 61, 82-83, 151-152
Maguire, John F. 42
Malcom, "Old" 52
Malcom's Chapel 35, 39, 52
Malou, Pierre 14, 17, 65-78, 79-91, 119, 145-148, 153-155, 159
Marcoux, Louis 55-56, 61-62
Maréchal, Ambrose 68, 77, 79, 83-86, 101, 143-149, 155
Masséna, André 28
Mazzetti, Guiseppe 81-87, 146-147, 154, 158
McKee, John 39

McMahon, Patrick 108-109, 111-112, 115-116, 131, 140-141, 152, 156
McNamara, Peter 106
McQuade, Paul 49-50, 55-63, 88, 101, 121, 141
Meteghan 62
Mignault, Pierre-Marie 45, 139
Milner, Dr John 26
Miramichi 13, 34-44, 49, 51-53, 59-60, 73, 75, 95-99, 106, 108, 113-114, 117, 121-122, 134, 140, 152, 155-156
Montauk Point (U.S.) 93
Morisset, Joseph 13, 51-53, 58, 61, 63-64, 73-74, 83, 84n.9, 88-89, 96, 100-101, 104, 114, 121, 134n.4, 136, 139-140, 142
Morris, Andrew 66, 68
Mountain, Jacob 34
Murphy, Nicholas 29-31, 75
Murphy, Terrence 138, 157

Neguac 35, 52, 97, 99, 152
Newport Light (U.S.) 93
Nipisiguit 98
Norton 37, 41, 61, 94
Nugent, Andrew 144n.33

O'Daniel, Victor 19-20, 72, 83n.8, 125n.21, 126n.22, 158-159n.10
O'Gallagher, Marianna 157
O'Gorman, Michael 66, 79

Panet, Bernard Claude 15, 84, 112-117, 122, 131, 135, 154
Passamaquoddy 61, 116-117
Patterson, James 124
Pius VI, Pope 153
Plessis, Joseph-Octave 13-15, 17, 26n.7, 33-54, 55-64, 68-78, 80-91, 95-96, 98-113, 119, 122, 130-148, 152-159

Index of Persons and Rural Localities   205

Portland (U.S.) 117-118
Portland Parish 103
Prevost, Sir George 34n.4

Raby, Louis 33, 74, 81-83
Richibucto 35, 45, 53, 134
Robichaud, Otho 97
Roux, Jean-Henri 67n.7

St. Andrew's 116-117, 134n.4
St. Antoine de Tilly 82
St. Basile 33, 55, 83n.7
Secord, William and Polly 41
Shaw, Dr 24
Signaÿ, Joseph 131-132
Sigogne, Jean-Mandé 62, 120-121
Simonds, Richard 44-45
Sinnot, John 56
Somaglia, Giulio 111
Sorbieu, Jean 146
Stack, James 96
Stoughton, Don Thomas 66
Sullivan, Andy 42
Swanton, Judge 96
Swiney [Sweeney], Fr 141

Tabusintac 35
Taylor, Mr 27
Taylor, William 66, 68, 79, 81,
    86-87, 93, 147
Têtu, Henri 151, 153
Toole, Garrett 49, 51
Toole, John 38, 51, 56-57, 61
Toole, Mary 95-96, 153, 155
Toole, Richard 73, 95
Toussaint, Pierre 146
Troy, John Thomas 26, 29-31

Walsh, Fr 140-141
Wellington, Duke of 28
Willcocks, Lewis 66, 68, 71-78,
    154-155

Zwierlein, Frederick 153-154

DR. LAWRENCE A. DESMOND taught Medieval History for some thirty-five years at St. Paul's College, University of Manitoba. A native of Saint John, New Brunswick, he now resides in Mississauga, Ontario.

DR. DONNA M. NORELL spent her teaching career on the faculty of the same College, in the Department of French, Spanish and Italian. She lives in Winnipeg.

Both retain the rank of Senior Scholar at St. Paul's College.